Winter War 1939–40

COMBAT

Finnish Soldier
VERSUS
Soviet Soldier

David Campbell

First published in Great Britain in 2016 by Osprey Publishing,
PO Box 883, Oxford, OX1 9PL, UK
1385 Broadway, 5th Floor, New York, NY 10018, USA
E-mail: info@ospreypublishing.com

Osprey Publishing, part of Bloomsbury Publishing Plc

A CIP catalogue record for this book is available from the British Library

Print ISBN: 978 1 4728 1324 4
PDF ebook ISBN: 978 1 4728 1325 1
ePub ebook ISBN: 978 1 4728 1326 8

Index by Rob Munro
Typeset in Univers, Sabon and Adobe Garamond Pro
Maps by bounford.com
Originated by PDQ Media, Bungay, UK
Printed in China through World Print Ltd.

16 17 18 19 20   10 9 8 7 6 5 4 3 2 1

Osprey Publishing supports the Woodland Trust, the UK's leading
woodland conservation charity. Between 2014 and 2018 our donations
are being spent on their Centenary Woods project in the UK.

www.ospreypublishing.com

Dedication

To David Greentree, for helping to kick-start the whole thing.

Acknowledgements

Thanks to Nik Cornish for his assistance with sourcing images of the Red
Army; to the Finnish Wartime Photograph Archive for their generous
and enlightened provision of historical images; to Graham Campbell for
technical support; to Dav Bisessar for his provision of a portable
technological device enclosure; to Geoff Banks for the smallest
measurable quotient of assistance; and of course to my editor Nick
Reynolds, who deserves better but is stuck with me.

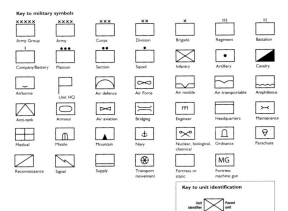

Comparative army ranks

US (1941)	Finnish	Soviet
General of the Army	Generalfeldmarschall	Komandarm or komanduyushchiy armii (Army Commander)
		Komandarm or komandarm vtorogo ranga (Army Commander of the second rank)
General	Sotomarsalkka	Komkor or komandír kórpusa (Corps Commander)
Lieutenant-General	Kenraali	Komdiv or komandír divízii (Division Commander)
Major-General	Kenraaliluutnantti	Kombrig or komandir brigady (Brigade Commander)
Brigadier-General	Kenraalimajuri	n/a
Colonel	Eversti	Polkóvnik
Lieutenant-Colonel	Everstiluutnantti	Podpolkóvnik (Sub-Colonel)
Major	Majuri	Mayór
Captain	Kapteeni	Kapitán
1st Lieutenant	Yliluutnantti	Stárshiy Leytenánt (Senior Lieutenant)
n/a	n/a	Leytenánt (Lieutenant)
2nd Lieutenant	Vänrikki	Mládshiy Leytenánt (Junior Lieutenant)
Sergeant-Major	Vääpeli, Sotilasmestari	Starshiná
Staff Sergeant	Ylikersantti	Stárshiy Serzhánt (Senior Sergeant)
Sergeant	Kersantti	Serzhánt
n/a	n/a	Mládshiy Serzhánt (Junior Sergeant)
Corporal	Alikersantti	n/a
Lance-corporal	Korpraali	Yefréytor
Private	Sotamies[1]	Ryadovóy, Krasnoarmeyets (Private, Red Army Man)

1. Sotamies (soldier); Kiväärimies (Rifleman); Tykkimies (Gunner); Pioneeri (Pioneer, Engineer)

CONTENTS

Introduction

The Russo-Finnish Winter War, which lasted for 105 days in the early months of World War II, would bring the Finns lasting international fame, while their Soviet foes would be marked with ignominy and opprobrium in equal measure. Almost from the first shots on 30 November 1939 until the Peace of Moscow treaty was signed on 12 March 1940 and implemented the following day, the conflict was cast as one of a plucky Nordic David against a belligerent Soviet Goliath, though one in which it was Goliath, bloodied and embarrassed, who would emerge the victor.

Finland was a part of the Russian Empire until 1917, when the Finns took their independence from the failing Tsarist regime. After a short civil war Finland emerged as an independent democratic republic, but it could not ignore the very obvious fact that its nearest neighbour to the east had an

A Finnish ski patrol returning across the border on 1 January 1940. Patrols such as these, which could spend days operating many kilometres behind Soviet lines in conditions that would be unsupportable for Soviet troops, were a constant worry for the Red Army and did much to secure the Finnish reputation for being able to hit anywhere at any time. The effects of such raids, coupled with the quick discovery that trees, villages, haystacks and even rivers and lakes had been booby-trapped, made the advancing Red Army units fearful and cautious, and encouraged them to stick closely to the existing road network – exactly where the Finns wanted them. (SA-kuva)

ideological and strategic disposition that was to pose a constant threat to the new nation's existence. Finland's system of defence, developed during the 1920s and 1930s, was built on the premise of the Soviet Union as the aggressor. Strategy and tactics were adapted to this unpleasant reality, despite the overwhelming disparity in size and military strength that existed between the two nations: Finland's population was around 3 million, that of the Soviet Union was 183 million; Finland's mobilized army (mostly made up of reservists of one stripe or another) numbered 337,000 men in total – nine divisions, three brigades and a number of independent battalions and units – while the standing Red Army numbered 1,600,000 men in no fewer than 98 divisions (though the initial Soviet assault would comprise only four armies). Surely the Finns, vulnerable and alone, would do anything to avoid the crushing reality of a war they realistically could not hope to win? For the Soviets, secure in their overwhelming power of arms, the idea that Finland would pursue any other option but acquiescence seemed wilfully absurd. Yet the Finns refused to bend: 'Finland preferred, if the choice had to be made, to die fighting rather than to accept the consequences of aggression, and she instructed her military technicians to prepare, within the limits of her natural resources, to sell the country as dearly as possible' (Langdon-Davies 1941: 6).

The initial cause of the conflict was the Soviet demand for a number of territorial and military concessions from the Finns; concessions that, despite their relatively small size, would effectively denude Finland of her main defensive capabilities in the Karelian Isthmus. To give what was asked for would have left Finland's future security dependent on the goodwill and honourable behaviour of her Soviet neighbour – characteristics that were demonstrably lacking after the violent partition of Poland only a few weeks

A rather ungainly Soviet patrol from January or February 1940. The Red Army's lack of preparation for war extended to the use of skis and camouflage, in which they were hopelessly outclassed by the Finns. Soviet scouts were sometimes issued with an 'amoeba'-pattern camouflage smock, but in the snow such items were not much more use than a greatcoat. By the beginning of 1940, Soviet forces were receiving warmer clothing as well as winter-camouflage outfits; the latter seemed to be either a one-piece 'boiler-suit' style that was awkward to wear and unpopular with the troops, or a voluminous white shroud of the type shown here that also left much to be desired. (Photo by ullstein bild/ullstein bild via Getty Images)

The British journalist and war correspondent John Langdon-Davies travelled to Finland in January 1940 to see the developing conflict for himself, and was struck by the nature of the landscape: 'I have travelled for miles through the type of country which the Russians found awaiting them. The roads are many miles apart. On both sides one is hemmed in by forest. The clearings for agricultural purposes are few and small. Every now and then a white, amorphous open space appears; finger-shaped and strangled in a noose of forest, it is one of Finland's 60,000 lakes. The country is not flat, neither is it hilly – a succession of confusing ups and downs, few of them possessing enough individuality to distinguish them from the rest. The roads themselves are beaten snow and solid ice … on either side of the road, marked very often by small uprooted saplings, begins a soft impassable waste which can only be negotiated on skis' (Langdon-Davies 1941: 10). By December, daylight only lasted for around five hours – and then only if the weather was clear – with snow lying 30cm or more deep on the iron-hard ground, and the temperature averaging -30°C and on occasion plummeting as low as -70°C.

Into this forbidding country four Soviet armies would make the attack: the 7th Army would strike into the Karelian Isthmus, aiming for Viipuri and after that Helsinki; the 8th Army would move through Ladoga–Karelia to turn the flank of the Finnish forces in the Isthmus; the 9th Army would cut the country in two by seizing Oulu on the Bothnian Gulf; and the 14th Army would take Petsamo in the far north. The Karelian Isthmus was the main point of attack. Army Commander (2nd rank) Vsevolod Fedorovich Yakovlev's 7th Army, tasked with breaking through the Finns' Karelian defences, consisted of two rifle and one tank corps – the 19th Rifle Corps was commanded by Division Commander Filipp N. Starikov, and the 50th Rifle Corps was commanded by Division Commander Filipp Danilovich Gorolenko, with the 10th Tank Corps in support: a total of 169,000 men, 1,490 tanks and 1,286 artillery pieces. Facing them were two Finnish corps – II Corps defending the right flank of the Isthmus including the route to Viipuri, and III Corps holding the left flank of the Isthmus along the Vuoksi River line. The two corps had six divisions and numerous smaller units between them, numbering around 133,000 men in all, though artillery was relatively scarce, and armour was to all intents and purposes non-existent. Ahead of this defensive line – soon to be christened the 'Mannerheim Line' – four delaying groups were positioned, comprised of 14 battalions and nine independent companies, from the south-west to the north-east: the Uusikirkko (U) Group, the Muolaa (M) Group, the Lipola (L) Group, and the Rautu (R) Group. Finnish defences in the rest of the country were sparse, and quite unprepared for the scale of the Soviet attack.

A Finnish machine-gun nest to the north of Lemetti, 21 February 1940 – note the large cap on the weapon's cooling jacket, a feature designed to allow snow to be used in lieu of water. In general the Winter War saw little of the atrocious brutality that would characterize the war with Germany, with Finns and Soviets retaining a sense of respect for each other, as well as an appreciation of each other's tactical capabilities. (SA-kuva)

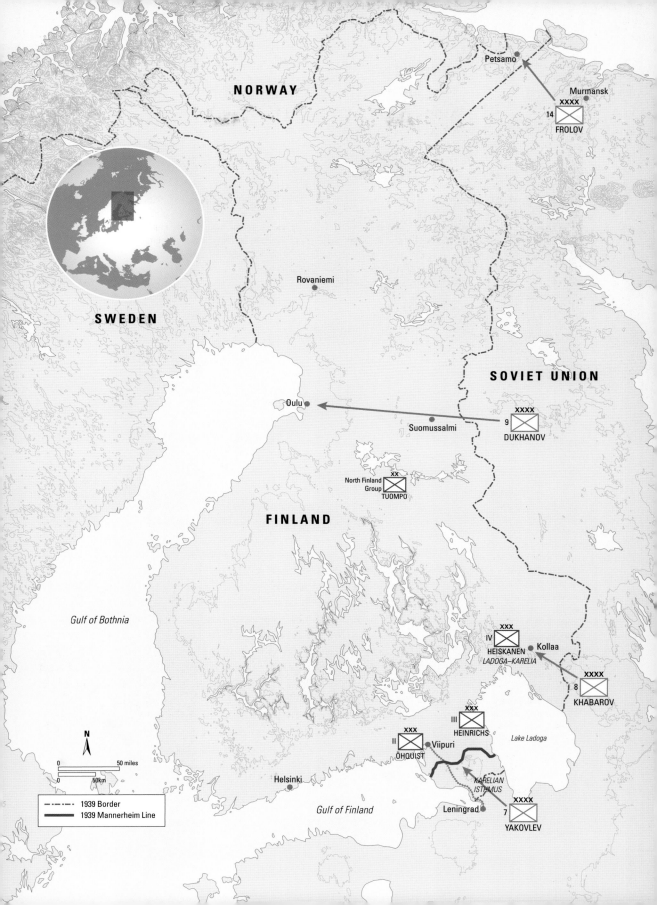

NORWAY

Petsamo

Murmansk

XXXX
14
FROLOV

SWEDEN

Rovaniemi

SOVIET UNION

Oulu

Suomussalmi

XXXX
9
DUKHANOV

North Finland
Group

XX
TUOMPO

FINLAND

Gulf of Bothnia

XXX
IV
HEISKANEN
LADOGA–KARELIA

Kollaa

XXXX
8
KHABAROV

XXX
III
HEINRICHS

Lake Ladoga

XXX
II
ÖHQUIST

Viipuri

KARELIAN
ISTHMUS

N

0   50 miles
0   50km

Helsinki

Gulf of Finland

Leningrad

XXXX
7
YAKOVLEV

------- 1939 Border
——— 1939 Mannerheim Line

Soviet vehicles in the aftermath of a Finnish attack. It was to be with a sense of increasing incredulity that international observers would watch the Red Army – one of the largest, most technologically advanced and impressive fighting forces anywhere in the world – grind its bones to a pulp in the depths of a Finnish winter in what would prove to be a terrible, traumatizing experience for the officers and men of the Red Army. (Nik Cornish at www.stavka.org.uk)

beforehand. The Soviet view – or more correctly Stalin's view – was driven by the desire to restore Russia's pre-1917 borders in the Baltic theatre, augmented by fears that the Finns would ally themselves with Hitler in the event of a German assault on the Soviet Union, thus making Leningrad vulnerable to attack from Finnish Karelia.

Stalin's diplomatic manoeuvrings were always to a certain degree a screen for his desire to swallow Finland whole, taking control of the entire country and running it through a tame puppet government. Thus it was that, when the Finns refused the opportunity to cede 11 per cent of their territory (including most of their major defensive lines and structures) to the Soviet Union, the shift from diplomatic to military pressure was almost instantaneous. The initial Soviet plan for war, put together in almost dismissive haste, envisaged a complete military victory in just 12 days (Reese 2011: 30). In a clumsily obvious manoeuvre that echoed Germany's excuse to commence war against Poland in September 1939, a Soviet border-guard post near the village of Mainila was shelled, with the attack blamed on the Finns. This wafer-thin pretext duly served as the justification for a massive Soviet invasion along the entire Soviet–Finnish border.

The Opposing Sides

ORGANIZATION AND DOCTRINE

Finnish

The Finnish armed forces had been developed in large part in the expectation of a war against the Soviet Union, and to this end two plans had been developed: Venäjän Keskitys (VK: Russian Concentration) 1 and 2. VK 1 was an aggressive plan that assumed a war against the Soviet Union while that power was simultaneously engaged in fighting with numerous foes across a broad front; VK 2 was more pessimistic, and concentrated on Finnish defence against Soviet incursions in the Karelian Isthmus and the area of Lake Ladoga (Irincheev 2011: 7). No serious thought had been given to defensive postures in the centre or north of the country, it being assumed that such avenues of attack were of low priority due to the difficult nature of the landscape and the limited gains on offer for an attacker.

Increasing tension between Finland and the Soviet Union throughout 1939 encouraged the Finns effectively to mobilize their Army, bringing its defensive lines up to strength. The historian Bair Irincheev notes the value of this early response to the impending crisis:

> Throughout October and November Finnish troops built additional fortifications and performed intensive combat training at squad-platoon-company-battalion level, with live ammunition firing and advanced tactics courses. Counter-attacks against Soviet breaches of the main defence line were rehearsed time and again. When war began, the main defence line was indeed home turf for Finnish troops: they knew every inch of the battlefield like their back garden. These two months of training and preparation played a crucial role in the battles of December 1939, largely contributing to the Soviet failure. (Irincheev 2011: 8)

The equipment issued to the Finnish soldier, from boots and brushes through to a gas mask, bayonet and axe. Needless to say, such largesse was rarely encountered by the Finns who scrambled to their reserve units in the months leading up to the Soviet invasion. Defence spending in Finland during the 1930s was as parsimonious and short-sighted as in most other countries, with the result that most soldiers were missing various items – approximately one-third had what they brought from home and little else. As most Finns possessed decent winter clothing, their own skis and often their own weapons, such shortages, though they may have been embarrassing for the Finnish Army, did not hinder units forming up in the short term. (SA-kuva)

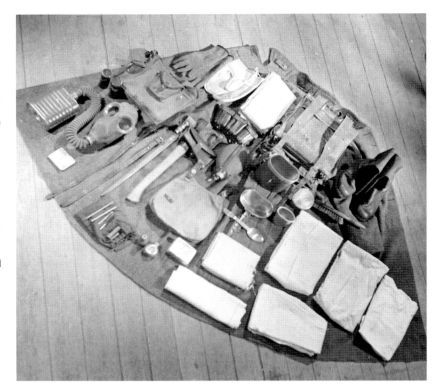

Finnish resources were limited. Artillery pieces were in short supply, with many guns dating from before World War I; air power was negligible (114 aircraft, a large number of which were old or obsolescent); there were only a handful of light tanks (20 obsolete Renault FT-17s that had been in Finnish service for 20 years and six Vickers Type E Alt Bs); radio and communications equipment was scarce; and there was a dearth of dedicated anti-tank weapons, there being only 50 37mm Bofors anti-tank guns and a small number of 20mm L39 Lahti anti-tank rifles for the whole Finnish Army at the outbreak of the war. In addition, ammunition was scarce, and supply was not expected to come anywhere near meeting demand in the first months of the war. As a result, Finland's Field Army was overwhelmingly an infantry force (six divisions and a cavalry brigade with covering forces in the Karelian Isthmus, two divisions north of Lake Ladoga, and another division's worth of reservists and border guards in the north), which would rely to a great extent on the nation's difficult and forbidding terrain and natural obstacles to maximize its defensive capabilities. The bulk of forces (II Corps and III Corps) would be deployed to the Karelian Isthmus, with strong forces (IV Corps) sited to the north of Lake Ladoga to frustrate any Soviet attempts to outflank the Karelian defences. Lands to the north were defended by the North Finland Group and a number of independent battalions.

The strategic reality the Finns faced was stark: they could fight a delaying war in the hope of outside help, or 'if that hope proved chimerical, the only thing left to do was resist so fiercely that Stalin would opt for a negotiated settlement rather than total conquest. If Stalin did seek total subjugation, the Finns would fight to the last man and bullet' (Trotter 2003: 39–40).

Soviet

Though it did not appear so, the Red Army was in a precarious state in 1939. The process of mechanization that had begun in the early 1930s, and which was meant to turn the Red Army into the world's foremost practitioner of armoured warfare, had been derailed, partly through indecisive and misinterpreted results from the Spanish Civil War of 1936–39, but mostly due to the fact that the main proponents of mechanization were ruthlessly purged from 1937 onwards.

A considerable amount of work had gone into understanding the new realities of warfare in the wake of World War I; indeed Soviet theories of operational art and deep battle, developed through the 1920s and 1930s, were ground-breaking in both their scope and audacity. Put succinctly, the Soviet vision was of highly mobile warfare in which massed tank forces supported by infantry, artillery and air power would conduct vast combined-arms assaults on the enemy's defensive line; a breakthrough battle would then develop seamlessly into a series of rolling sequential operations that exploited the breakthrough, with echeloned waves driving deep into the enemy's rear areas, attacking key targets and giving him no time to recover or organize any effective resistance.

By the time *Vremenny Polevoy Ustav RKKA 1936* (*Provisional Field Regulations for the Red Army 1936*; more commonly referred to as PU-36) was published, Soviet offensive doctrine was well developed: 'The emphasis throughout PU-36 was on speed, audacity, seizing the initiative at all levels, and the aggressive use of their own initiative by subordinate commanders at all levels' (Kagan 2002: 91). Unfortunately, the Red Army lacked the training,

A Finn fires his 7.62mm Lahti-Saloranta M/26 light machine gun (LMG) next to a bunker on the Kollaa front, 17 December 1939. The M/26 was the main Finnish LMG of the war, but it was never available in the required quantities and increasing numbers of captured 7.62mm DP-28 LMGs were also used by Finnish troops. Using a 20-round magazine the M/26 could fire on semi- or full automatic (at 450–550 rounds per minute); ammunition was carried in bags that could take five or ten magazines apiece, with each M/26-equipped LMG squad issued with up to 90 magazines in total. (SA-kuva)

The figure shown is a Finnish infantryman from III/IR 29, a member of a reconnaissance patrol sent out to determine the size and seriousness of the Soviet incursion onto the Finnish side of the Suvanto waterway in the early hours of Christmas Day. He wears a well-weathered snowsuit over his uniform and carries a 9mm Suomi KP/31 submachine gun; a division was issued around 250 KP/31s for around 14,000 men, only enough for each rifle squad to have one Suomi-armed soldier, but a soldier who was specifically trained in the gun's use. Such gunners quickly became known as *Tikkakosken mannekiinit* ('Tikkakoski mannequins') for their distinctive appearance, and had an impact out of all proportion to their numbers.

Weapons, dress and equipment

Most Finns would be armed with a Finnish variant of the 7.62mm Mosin-Nagant rifle, but submachine guns, though not available in nearly enough numbers, were also important weapons; the soldier shown here is armed with the 9mm Suomi KP/31 submachine gun (**1**) built at the Tikkakoski factory and fed by a 70-round 'Koskinen' drum magazine, a spare of which hangs from his belt by a piece of string (**2**) as there were no official pouches produced for carrying extra drum ammunition. He is also armed with a Varsikranaatti M32 hand grenade (**3**), basically the same weapon as the German M24 'potato-masher' but with a heavily knurled fuse cap and a clip to make it easier to carry; he also carries a *puukko* knife (**4**), a common and highly individual tool-cum-weapon that every soldier supplied himself, meaning that though the knives had a common design they came in all shapes and sizes.

His snowsuit (**5**) is a two-piece model, though there were many variations in style and design as such camouflage items were often home-made, sometimes simply by cutting a neck-hole in a white sheet. He wears the enlisted man's fur cap (**6**) with blue-and-white pressed-steel cockade (officers would have the same style in enamel or a gold lion on an red enamel background), as well as 'Lapp' boots (**7**) that were specially designed for use with skis; such boots were issued by the Army but many men had their own, and equipment shortages meant that home-supplied items were not uncommon. He carries a rucksack that is camouflaged with a cover made from a sheet (**8**) as well as a bread bag (**9**) that would be used for food, medical supplies, spare ammunition and anything else the soldier might need. His equipment with pack comes to around 18–23kg.

Red Army soldiers, including a DP-28 LMG team. Note the M-36 backpacks, soon to be superseded by the more practical 1938 model. To be a Soviet soldier in the years before the outbreak of the Winter War was to be part of a strange, paranoid machine in which on the one hand absolute loyalty and trust were demanded of the men, while on the other they regularly saw their officers removed or dismissed for supposedly treasonable offences. The historian Roger R. Reese notes how 'The effect of the purge was not only to remove many competent officers but to create an air of distrust among the officers and their men, who, influenced by state-controlled media propaganda, became predisposed to believe that their commander could be a traitor or a spy' (Reese 2014: 45). (Nik Cornish at www.stavka.org.uk)

equipment and ethos to convert that doctrine into anything approaching reality – a situation made immeasurably worse by the purges of 1937 that effectively removed all proponents of such warfare from the Red Army. By the time of the Winter War the Soviet approach had reverted to the belief that 'the correct way to win a modern battle was through a slow, methodical advance by masses of foot soldiers, closely supported by artillery, aircraft, and tanks that would act as little more than moving shields' (Habeck 2002: 101–02).

The shift away from deep battle occurred at a time when the Red Army was beginning a process of massive expansion – from 1.3 million men in 1937 to 4.5 million men by 1941. The stresses that such a vast undertaking put on recruitment, training and organization meant that the Red Army's old failings – 'indiscipline, rampant alcoholism, equipment and weapon shortages, and inattentiveness to training' (Reese 2014: 43) – were greatly exacerbated. In the 12 weeks before the outbreak of the Winter War, some of the units meant to

A pair of Soviet soldiers manhandle a 7.62mm PM M1910 Maxim machine gun set on a wheeled Sokolov mount with defensive plate attached. The gun weighed in at 24kg on its own, the mount and armoured plate adding another 43.5kg for a total (excluding ammunition) of 67.5kg. The example shown here has been jury-rigged onto a pair of skis, though the gun's weight would have made for hard work even with such an amendment: the armoured ski sledges developed by the Soviets in the later stages of the war were of a similar weight, and they had a tendency to bog down in snow. By contrast, Finnish soldiers used sledges to move their Maxims. They also tended to leave off the armoured plate, its extra weight not usually being considered worth the small degree of protection it offered. Those soldiers who chose to retain the plate were advised not to fix it to the gun carriage too tightly – the subtle looseness seemed to make the plate more effective in deflecting bullets. (Courtesy of the Central Museum of the Armed Forces, Moscow via Stavka)

be part of the invasion force were still being formed, with drafts of men and officers assigned first here, then there; in such forces the officers and men were virtually unknown to one another, and had almost no chance to overcome such ignorance as there was no time for training or exercises, leading to obvious problems of unit cohesion and weak leadership. Generally poor organization was compounded by poor cooperation between battalion-sized units, with similar failings between the infantry and armour – problems that had been clearly identified after the Red Army's clashes with Japanese forces at Lake Khasan and Khalkin-Gol during the Soviet–Japanese border conflicts of 1938–39 (Reese 1996: 169–70), but about which nothing had been done.

RECRUITMENT AND MORALE

Finnish

In the early 1930s, Finland moved towards a regional recruitment model to support the standing army and allow for faster mobilization in time of war. The majority of Finnish reserve units were raised in local areas, resulting in easy familiarity and comradeship as the men often knew one another in civilian life. Independent battalions and other such units were mostly raised from the border areas. Upon reaching the age of 18, men were liable for conscription (350 days for enlisted men; 440 days for NCOs and officers), and were subject to recall at intervals for refresher training that was conducted in a number of regional centres based around the country. In addition, the Civic Guard (Suojeluskunnat), a Finnish youth organization similar in some ways to the Komsomol (the youth organization of the Communist Party of the Soviet Union), played an important role in preparing young men for military service, though this was not its principal aim.

A Finnish tent in the area near Suomussalmi, 1 December 1939. Such tents would quickly prove their worth, providing shelter, warmth and hot food for weary Finnish soldiers on their way from their more permanent wooden bunkers to and from the front line. Often located relatively close to the front, the tents allowed a regular rotation of troops and helped to ensure that frostbite and problems caused by exposure to the elements were kept to a minimum, as well as keeping morale high. For the most part the Soviets endured the diametrical opposite of the Finnish experience, often huddled in the open, with no hot food available, knowing that any attempt to warm themselves by open fires would bring sniper fire and mortar rounds down upon them. (SA-kuva)

OPPOSITE A sheaf of Soviet propaganda leaflets, one of many, found on the battlefield at Lemetti in January 1940. Most Politruks enjoyed a pedestrian existence, for example helping men with personal issues while organizing tedious sessions of indoctrination for the soldiers under their care. Part of such indoctrination was a concerted effort to paint the Finns as villains in the run-up to the Winter War; and there is plenty of evidence that the propaganda put about as the reason for the invasion – that the White Finns were the aggressors, and that the Red Army was coming to the rescue of deprived and persecuted Finnish workers – was effective, with most Soviet soldiers thinking it was a just war. Even after the cold reality of the first month's disasters had disabused most Soviet troops of the idea that they would be welcomed as liberators, there remained a belief that they were doing the right thing for the right reasons, so ingrained was their sense of purpose. (SA-kuva)

Morale was strong, in part due to the good training and cohesive nature of Finnish military organization, but augmented by a strong sense of national identity that was heightened by the prospect of foreign invasion. Langdon-Davies had an illuminating discussion with a Finnish communist about his priorities in a war with the Soviet Union:

> When I asked what he felt about the war and about communism, he replied, 'These are not the times for political discussions, but one thing I will say: I have always understood that revolution was a thing that came from within, whereas war is a thing that comes from without. As a communist, therefore, I believe that communist Russia is wrong to attack us; and that my duty is to help defend the workers of Finland against attack from without.' (Quoted in Langdon-Davies 1941: 193)

Soviet

The Red Army's soldiers were drawn from the workers and peasants, the former usually ending up in technical and mechanized units, while the latter made up the overwhelming bulk of the rifle regiments. Men were conscripted at the age of 19 in military districts for two years of active duty.

Recruitment of officers proved problematic. The traditional source of recruitment (the bourgeoisie and aristocracy) was unthinkable, such class enemies being forbidden to enlist or be conscripted, so it was the workers and peasants that were the main wells upon which the Red Army had to draw. As Reese observes, however, these societal groups had no military tradition, and were not overly enamoured of the prospect of Army life anyway, soldiers having relatively low status in the Soviet Union (Reese 1996: 130). By the time of the 1937 purges there were 10,000 unfilled junior officer posts – a

Stalin, in the company of Kliment Yefremovich Voroshilov, the People's Commissar for Defence. Voroshilov was a strong believer that any war with the Finns would be quick and decisive, due to internal Finnish political weakness as well as the Red Army's overwhelming strength. Maintaining Soviet morale in the face of what quickly proved to be a terrible, vicious conflict was difficult. Even so, relatively few Soviet soldiers cut and ran, and only small numbers were taken prisoner (around 5,486 throughout the whole war). More often units seemed to retain their integrity, fighting together until they were overrun or finally broke. The initial disasters of the war, which saw Soviet units sometimes forced to retreat in the face of orders, caused consternation within Stavka (the high command of the armed forces), which organized the formation of rear-echelon units to catch and punish fleeing soldiers. However, 'Even Stalin, for all his ruthlessness and cynicism, recognized that there were limits to the use of heavy-handed methods. The key methods used by Soviet authorities to keep the men fighting were appeals to patriotism and duty, based on portrayals of the war as just and necessary, and brutal but selective punishment of noncompliance, desertion and cowardice' (Reese 2011: 54). (Nik Cornish at www.stavka. org.uk)

shortage that was compounded by the purges as well as by the rapid expansion of the Red Army initiated that same year. Those junior officers that could be found underwent a truncated training regimen of one to two years, with many only completing six months of education, as opposed to the four years that was usual prior to 1937. Such men found themselves ill-equipped when moved into positions of responsibility, with little help from above (where similar problems existed) or below, where the traditional Russian disdain for NCOs was exacerbated by further significant personnel shortages. The job of maintaining morale, both military and political, fell to the Politruks (political officers) and Commissars who were assigned to every unit from rifle companies upward. Such men had once again become a fact of life in the Red Army as a result of the purges, their duty being to ensure political reliability through joint command.

TRAINING, TACTICS AND WEAPONRY

Finnish

Most Finnish recruits (around 70 per cent) were drawn from rural areas, and many were accomplished hunters and woodsmen. Such backgrounds and experience made for fine soldiers – especially ones that had to live and fight in Finland's winter-wrapped forests. Finnish soldiers, trained for and expecting to fight a defensive battle within their country's borders, were prepared to make the most of the battlefield.

Considerable care was taken in the provision of shelter and hot food, a common practice among Finnish patrols or forces moving towards staging points in preparation for an attack being to lay up in specially constructed dugouts or tents. Stoves were small, easily portable and reliable – in stark contrast to the great bulk of the Soviet field kitchens that so quickly became targets for Finnish snipers and mortarmen. Clothing was rugged and practical, with felt-lined boots designed to be worn in conjunction with skis, and snow smocks (either issued or often home-made) for camouflage. Large loads, such as supplies, ammunition or crew-served weapons, were transported on a *pulka*, a low-lying toboggan that looked rather like a flat-bottomed canoe and which could be pulled by a man, or on an *ahkio* (a larger version of the *pulka*). Larger loads were pulled on a horse-drawn *ackja* sledge, though such transport was best-suited to travel over 'winter' or 'ice' roads.

The tactics developed by the Finns were adapted to the landscape in which they fought, as well as to the weapons they had at their disposal and the habits of their enemy. When the opportunity presented itself, as it did several times in the battles around Suomussalmi and the Raate Road, the Finns would look

to engage in a *motti* battle, in which the aim was to pin down an enemy force, cutting it up and defeating the parts in detail, as noted by General der Infanterie Waldemar Erfurth, the Wehrmacht liaison officer to the Finns throughout the Continuation War (1941–44): 'Finnish tactics aim to penetrate the front of the enemy, to separate the enemy's strong points from each other, to cut off these strong points completely from all arteries of supply, and to encircle them' (Erfurth 1951: 19). Once the enemy forces were pinned the Finns used their mobility to outflank Soviet positions, maintaining pressure on them with constant sniping and hit-and-run attacks, finally launching surprise assaults that were designed to cut the enemy line into several well-contained segments and then wear them down with harassing fire, thus provoking them into futile and costly counter-attacks.

The Finnish hit-and-run attacks could be especially potent because of the judicious use of 9mm Suomi KP/31 submachine guns. Though never issued in very large numbers (250 per division), the KP/31 SMG was usually entrusted to a man trained in its use, often a squad leader. Grenades, home-made bombs and Molotov cocktails were also used whenever an attack pushed close enough to a Soviet position. Though most Finns carried variants of the 7.62mm Mosin-Nagant M1891 rifle, they did not have much recourse to the bayonet, especially while on skis; illustrations of bayonet fighting on skis shown in *Ski-Training in the RKKA* demonstrate Soviet inexperience in this area, as the manoeuvres shown (including bayonet lunges and bayonet-to-bayonet close combat) would be wildly impractical if actually tried in the real world. Langdon-Davies noted that the Finns did not use their bayonets, either on skis or off them, in part because

> the bayonet is by no means a suitable weapon for forest fighting. Orthodox infantry manuals … point out candidly that the effectiveness of a bayonet charge is largely psychological. A bayonet charge, accompanied by the barbaric whoop prescribed in our training instructions, is a most unpleasant sight for the enemy. It is ideal in certain circumstances in open country: but where visibility is poor and silence [is] a more powerful asset than the most terrifying noise, the bayonet is poor stuff. (Langdon-Davies 1941: 23)

The weapon of choice, carried by every Finn, was the *puukko* knife. Langdon-Davies again:

> The place of the bayonet is taken in Finnish practice by the *puukko* … it has a straight blade seven and a half inches [19cm] long, tapering to a point in the last inch and a half [3.8cm]. Its handle is four and a half inches [11.4cm] long and made of polished wood. It is enclosed in a scabbard of tooled leather shaped like

Finnish radio sports commentator Pekka Tiilikainen photographed with examples of Soviet and Finnish skis side by side (the Soviet ski is the smaller one on the right). '"You can always tell a Russian skier," a Finnish soldier said to me. "If you see a man walking along the road with a pair of skis on his back, that is a Russian skier"' (quoted in Langdon-Davies 1941: 29). Dmitrii A. Krutskikh, a lieutenant with the Soviet 54th Mountain Rifle Division, had first-hand experience of the shortcomings of Soviet ski equipment: 'Let's compare, for instance, our skis and the Finnish ones. Our skis didn't have "peksas" – sewn-on toe pockets but had to be tied up with straps. To dismount the skis, one had to untie the straps, to mount – tie them up. Too much hassle. When airplanes dropped valenkis [felt boots] for us, we sewed balls on and slid the foot straight under the arch' (Krutskikh Interview). (SA-kuva)

3

2

1

The figure shown is an infantryman from II/220 RR running across the frozen waters of the Suvanto waterway during the early-morning hours of 25 December. Like many of his fellow soldiers he is poorly dressed for the conditions, lacking winter boots or *valenki* felt boots, though he is armed with a 6.5mm Fedorov Avtomat rifle, a weapon designed in World War I and a precursor to the 7.62mm SVT-38 rifle borne by some of his contemporaries. His battalion, together with the scout company from the 101st Rifle Regiment, will make it across the ice undetected, allowing them to establish a bridgehead on the Finnish bank of the river near Kelja. Other attempted crossings at Volossula and Patoniemi will be beaten back by the Finns in short order, leaving the Soviets at Kelja alone in the enemy's lines.

4

5

Weapons, dress and equipment

The Red Army man pictured here has been lucky enough to trade in his 7.62mm Mosin-Nagant M/91-30 rifle for a 6.5mm Fedorov Avtomat (**1**), a relic of the Russian Civil War that was quickly brought back into service to provide more automatic weapons for the soldiers fighting on the Karelian Isthmus; the rifle could fire in fully automatic mode but would overheat fairly quickly in constant use, and at 5.2kg it was not a light weapon. Some 2,000–3,000-odd Fedorovs were still in storage and the entire stock was consumed in the Winter War. The Fedorov used 25-round detachable box magazines, but the pouches available (e.g. for the Mosin-Nagant or the SVT-38) were too small for them, so spare ammunition would most likely be carried in his gas mask bag. He also carries a grenade pouch (**2**) with two F1 'Limonka' hand grenades, probably supplied to him just before the current attack as there were often shortages of such weapons and ammunition generally.

The soldier wears a *budenovka* (**3**), still very common despite the move towards issuing more troops with M-36 'Kaska' or the newer SSh-39 steel helmets; his greatcoat (**4**) is not good enough to deal with the harsh winter weather of the campaign, and the issue of the *telogreika* (padded jacket) and *vatni sharovari* (padded trousers) to infantry was poor in the initial months of the war. His boots and puttees (**5**) are totally inadequate for the conditions in which he is fighting, and such insufficiencies caused many needless casualties from frostbite. He carries an M/1939 pack (**6**) with groundsheet, an entrenching tool (**7**) that would double as a close-combat weapon, a water-bottle (**8**) and a BN gas mask bag (**9**) that was often used for carrying any number of items or foodstuffs in lieu of the actual gas mask. His weapon, ammunition and equipment comes to around 20–25kg.

A Finnish team prepare to fire their 81mm Krh/33 mortar from their dugout on the Kollaa front, 1 February 1940. The mortar was a simple and effective weapon that was used to great effect in a war in which more substantial forms of artillery support were usually lacking. Enemy ordnance was often pressed into service almost as soon as it was captured in an attempt to make up for the dire shortfall in domestic supply. The Krh/33, the first of the Finnish-made mortars, had a range of up to 2,700m and could fire up to 30 rounds per minute, making it an excellent weapon for quick, devastating attacks on encircled Soviet positions at Raate, Suomussalmi and Lemetti. (SA-kuva)

a reindeer's antlers … It is exceedingly difficult to discover how far this weapon is actually used in warfare. I have met sceptics among foreign observers who deny that it is used at all. But I have been told by Finnish soldiers, as a matter of technical interest and with no boastfulness, that they have knifed a whole machine-gun crew, and captured the gun, armed with nothing but their *puukkos*. (Langdon-Davies 1941: 23–24)

Finnish officers read Soviet ski manuals taken from the hoards of booty captured at Suomussalmi. The manuals, with their carefully drawn diagrams showing, for example, how to fire one's rifle or engage in a bayonet fight while still on one's skis, left the Finns incredulous. Errors started with instructions on how to attach skis to one's boots, and got progressively worse from there. When shown proposed Soviet tactics that included ferrying men into battle dragged on skis behind horses or motorcycles, a Finnish patrolman noted that 'you don't beat an enemy by thinking up clever ideas like that. What counts is being able to go out on ski patrol for three days and nights in a temperature of thirty below zero and be able to fight as well at the end of that time as the beginning' (quoted in Langdon-Davies 1941: 28). (SA-kuva)

Soviet

As war with Finland loomed, the Soviet leadership began its hasty preparations for the coming conflict, rushing into print *Ski-Training in the RKKA* in October–November 1939 while talks to avoid war were still under way. It was a good example of just how little the Red Army understood about the war it had decided to fight, as Langdon-Davies observed:

> I have learned all I know about ski-fighting by availing myself of every opportunity to show a copy of this manual to stray Finnish soldiers met in trains and restaurants, and listening to their criticisms … The Russian Ski Manual has evidently been compiled by a pure theoretician. Much of its advice would be excellent for tourists at a Swiss winter sports centre … The Russian Manual shows skis fitted with the various forms of heel-straps. No Finn would ever have a heel-strap fitted to his skis, since his safety and efficiency depend upon his being able to kick off his skis in an instant of time … every Finnish soldier who saw the book at once exclaimed at this elementary error. (Langdon-Davies 1941: 19)

Such a basic failing was indicative of the whole Soviet approach to the war. The infantry and mechanized units had no experience of (or specialist training in) winter tactics or fighting in densely forested landscapes. Artillery support, traditionally one of the most dominating features of the Red Army, was hamstrung by a lack of howitzers and often – such as on the Raate Road – by diminished use because the close terrain denied the guns effective fields of fire. Weapons and machinery were ill-adapted to functioning in the sub-zero temperatures of an arctic winter. Added to these failings was the most egregious omission – the lack of proper winter clothing for the majority of Soviet troops. Felt boots, padded jackets, white snow smocks and mittens were just some of the items desperately needed but generally unavailable. Such shortages would be rectified to some extent after the horrendous losses of December 1939 and

Soviet infantry attack across open ground during the Winter War. Soviet doctrine was clear that 'The infantry, in close cooperation with the artillery and the armored vehicles, decides the outcome of an engagement by resolute conduct in the attack' (PU-36 1986: 3), and yet the military theorist and historian Basil Liddell Hart observed that the Red Army's handling of infantry formations was clumsily old-fashioned: '[infantry] formations are apt to offer too good a target. The unique disregard of the effects of modern fire … seemed to invite casualties needlessly' (quoted in Langdon-Davies 1941: 104). The old habit of battalions charging en masse was still being seen at the end of the war, in part because Army Commander (1st rank) Semyon Konstantinovich Timoshenko, commander of the North-Western Front, had little sentimentality for the lives of his men; he knew that attrition, however grim it might be for his own forces, would become unsustainable far quicker for the Finns. (Courtesy of the Central Museum of the Armed Forces, Moscow via Stavka)

A Red Army gun crew, January or February 1940. The men are serving a 76mm Schneider M1909 mountain gun, readily identifiable by its curved shield. The artillerymen shown here are well dressed for the conditions, with mittens, fleece-lined coats and *valenki* felt boots; most wear the M-36 'Kaska' steel helmet, apart from the loader who appears to be sporting the more modern SSh-39. (Photo by ullstein bild/ullstein bild via Getty Images)

early January 1940, but tens of thousands of casualties resulted from the Red Army's unconscionably poor planning. The particular problems associated with conducting infantry operations in deep winter were not unknown to the Red Army, as clearly, if nominally, laid out in their own regulations:

> The mobility and maneuverability of the troops in winter depends entirely upon their training, their winter equipment, and the terrain of the winter battlefield. Troops not trained and insufficiently equipped for winter operations quickly lose their combat capability, and equipment not adapted for winter use only serves to become a burden to them. If such deficiencies are detected in the enemy, they must be resolutely and tirelessly used for his defeat. (PU-36 1986: 93)

Training within one's unit was the main method of military education for Soviet soldiers, but there was great variation from unit to unit. Officers were responsible for the effective training of their men, from divisional commanders down to platoon officers, but they could be idiosyncratic as to how they went about this. In addition, the general increase in the size of the Red Army together with the effect of the purges resulted in a considerable reduction in the competence of officers at every level, resulting in commensurately poor training regimens for the men under their care. Basic instruction in cover, fire and movement, weapons, small-unit tactics and cooperation with artillery and armour were supposed to be covered, but there was no comprehensive way for the Red Army to measure how effectively its men had absorbed such lessons – or indeed if they had been taught them at all. Training time was also often circumscribed by other civic priorities, including grain harvests, which could take soldiers away from their training routines for weeks at a time.

One of the more unusual developments of the war was the armoured ski sledge, a Soviet innovation that was meant to be drawn behind advancing tanks. One tank officer, Aleksey Shilin, saw them in action: 'In the meantime the command decided to try another attack with "infantry tanks" that had been rushed out of the factories. They called it a "tank" because it was made from a panel of twelve millimetre thick armour, equipped with a firing hole for rifles … and an observation slit for the soldier, so he could watch where he was going. The whole structure was mounted on skis and weighed more than eighty kilogrammes. Now, just think, the developers quite seriously believed that by equipping our units with these things we would be able to encircle the Mannerheim Line. Of course, life doesn't work out that way. The skis bearing the "infantry tanks" sank foot-deep in the snow. Many of my friends were killed then. I especially remember one severely wounded soldier, still alive, trying and failing to smother the pain in his face with his hands' (Shilin Memoir). (SA-kuva)

The effect of such failings would prove costly. In the Karelian battles, Soviet commanders often resorted to massed charges, attempting to overwhelm their enemy by sheer weight of numbers, their formations being used as blunt, bloodied battering rams. In the treacherous snows of Ladoga–Karelia and on the narrow forest roads in the north, Soviet formations had no room to fight set-piece mechanized battles; tanks and artillery often could not be brought to bear when and where they were most needed because it was not physically possible to move them through vehicle-heavy divisional columns that had turned into traffic jams kilometres long. The brunt of the fighting fell to the infantry; and considering their general poverty in training, the frequent lack of artillery or armoured support, the harsh operating environment, the shortages of food, ammunition and winter clothing, and the poor leadership to which they were subject, most Red Army infantry units fought with a considerable degree of vigour, exhibiting a stubborn determination that impressed the Finns far more than it did their own commanders.

LEADERSHIP AND COMMUNICATIONS

Finnish

The most significant aspect of the Finnish officer corps was the role played in its development by men who had served together as volunteers in Königlich Preussisches Jäger-Bataillon Nr. 27 of the Imperial German Army during World War I. A significant number of Finnish commanders in the Winter War had served in the battalion, and brought their battle-hardened competence to subsequent engagements with their Soviet opponents. Sergeant Pekka Niemi, a Finnish cross-country ski champion before the Winter War, spoke of how 'our troops are well trained and well led. Many of our officers served in the German or Russian armies in the old days. Finland's forests and lakes make it easy for us to block enemy advances. On skis we can glide through the forests to cut them up from the flanks like firewood' (quoted in Bull 2013: 12).

The generally strong sense of nationhood and purpose that could be found throughout the Finnish rank and file was also present within the officer corps, Langdon-Davies noting 'the ease and comradeship existing between officers and men, both at the front and, more surprisingly, at the rear' (Langdon-Davies 1941: 173). He saw two main reasons for such unity: first, Finland was not a class-conscious nation in peacetime, so some of the artificial social barriers that separate officers from their men were not as strong; and second, he thought there were higher levels of technical skill needed in the Finnish Army, so there was no temptation to see the men as a faceless, uneducated horde.

Finnish units went to war with a shortage of good telephone cable – a shortage quickly exacerbated by the depredations of Soviet artillery fire that cut and re-cut the existing lines. As a result, some units were forced to rely upon civilian telephone networks for their communications. Radios were also in desperately short supply; Finland had classified its field radio requirements as follows: corps-level (AB-), divisional-level (B-), sub-unit level (C-) and artillery (D-). At the start of the war there were only 239 B-, C- and D-Radio sets available in the whole country, and though there were frenzied attempts to buy in foreign stocks from France, Sweden and Hungary, all but a handful failed to arrive in Finland until after the war was over. Captured Soviet equipment was much prized, with 165 radio sets taken from vehicles or infantry units being pressed into service by the Finns throughout the war.

A Finnish captain in discussion with another officer, both of them well dressed for war in the arctic north. Note the distinctive decorated fur mittens as well as the leggings: good examples of personal civilian garments that were brought to the front by their owners. (SA-kuva)

A typical Finnish night patrol in the area of Summa, 14 December 1939. Note the Varsikranaatti M32 stick grenade on the left-hand soldier's belt – it was very similar to the German M24 Stielhandgranate, the only real differences being a slightly different design for the grenade cap (the German version was plain; the Finnish version was knurled to give the user better purchase, especially when wearing gloves) and the addition of a clip to the grenade's charge, making the M32 easier to carry on a belt (as shown here). (SA-kuva)

Soviet

From the middle of 1937 the Red Army's officer corps was effectively destroyed by the Soviet state it was sworn to serve. By late 1939 the job of healing such grievous and self-inflicted wounds in the Red Army's leadership was nowhere near complete, with serious deficiencies in experience, competence and professionalism at every level. Leadership problems ran from the platoon all the way up the chain of command, as observed by Commissar Semionov of the 50th Rifle Corps who stated that 'Regiments and divisions were sometimes given to incompetent, inexperienced and poorly trained people who failed at the slightest difficulty in battle' (quoted in Reese 2011:

A Soviet officer wearing a *telogreika* padded jacket instructs a pair of scouts, most likely in early 1940. Relations between Red Army officers and their subordinates were meant to be comradely and defined by mutual respect, and sometimes this was indeed the case, as noted by Lieutenant Dmitrii Krutskikh: 'We were just friends with my subordinates. There were people of many nations, we lived close and merrily. But we didn't have any relations expressly proscribed by the Service Regulations. The soldiers took care of me. Everything was in the open. Any rowdiness by an officer would end up by his death in the first combat. I have no doubt about that. As far as our command, we had a good relationship with our battalion commander. This was the guy who led us in combat, along with his staff commander and commissar' (Krutskikh Interview). The 'rowdiness' referred to by Krutskikh has been identified as physical abuse of one's soldiers (Reese 2008: 839), something not uncommon in the Soviet armed forces of the time (or subsequently). (Courtesy of the Central Museum of the Armed Forces, Moscow via Stavka)

42). Officers in charge of platoons and companies were generally undertrained – a combination of the purges and the Red Army's rapid expansion meant training courses were truncated in order to fill the growing gaps in the junior officer corps – resulting in 'a lack of practical experience and inability to train their platoons during field training [that] constituted the gravest problem for line units' (Reese 1996: 164). The NCO corps, the backbone of most Western armies, was mostly absent within the Red Army. There had never been a strong tradition of leadership from below; and in the wake of the Russian Revolution of 1917, NCOs as a concept were ideologically undesirable, reinforcing as they did the disparity in rank and privilege between the masses and their bourgeois or aristocratic overlords. Thus terms like 'Junior Commander' were preferred.

Command and control was primarily meant to operate through encoded radio networks, with particular attention paid to the use of radios in reconnaissance units as well as an early-warning 'nervous system' that could alert a division and any neighbouring units to enemy incursions. Such radio communications were vulnerable to interception, however, with the Finns making great use of intercepted Soviet radio traffic, often reading decoded messages within a matter of hours of their original transmission. Some messages were even easier to deal with as they were sent uncoded – a practice that had been noted during the Soviet Union's border conflicts with Japan. Rifle regiments had a dedicated signals company (a signals battalion for divisions) to manage all their radio and telephone communications, though runners were still used extensively. In T-26 light infantry and BT-7 light cavalry tanks radios were only usually installed in command vehicles, with flares, flags and hand signals used to communicate between most vehicles.

The Taipale Sector

6–27 December 1939

BACKGROUND TO BATTLE

The Soviet attack, when it came, was massive, involving the whole of Finland from its southern flank to its northernmost tip, but the main strength of the Red Army was clearly thrown at the Karelian Isthmus. The objective of the southern thrust was to punch a hole right through the Finnish defences and seize Viipuri, then move on from there to Helsinki. The job was given to the freshly formed 7th Army commanded by Army Commander (2nd rank) Vsevolod Fedorovich Yakovlev and assembled in Leningrad on 14 September, only six weeks before the invasion). After a furious artillery barrage the 7th Army's two rifle corps marched across the Finnish border on the morning of 30 November, accompanied by their marching bands in full swing. Division Commander Filipp N. Starikov's 19th Rifle Corps was to capture Viipuri by penetrating the 'Viipuri Gateway', a tract of passable land that lay on the western flank of the Isthmus, while the 50th Rifle Corps under Division Commander Filipp Danilovich Gorolenko was to advance on Käkisalmi on the north-eastern side of the Isthmus.

The Finnish forces were arrayed along a series of defensive positions that ran from the Gulf of Finland to Lake Ladoga – soon to be christened by the world's press as the Mannerheim Line – Lieutenant-General Harald Öhquist's II Corps on the right flank, with Major-General Erik Heinrichs' III Corps on the left. Four delaying groups (Uusikirkko, Muolaa, Lipola and Rautu: U, L,

A lone Finnish sentry stands guard by a ferry terminal on the Taipale River, 1 December 1939. The strength of the Soviet attack justified the Finnish decision to draw back from defending the majority of the Koukkunniemi promontory. The ground was marshy and difficult for tanks, but the coming frosts would soon harden the swamps and even render the river surfaces solid enough to support men and vehicles in significant numbers. (SA-kuva)

M and R) were positioned ahead of the main defensive line in the hope that they would be able to blunt the initial force of the Soviet attack. To augment the impact of the delaying force minefields had been laid, booby traps set, and snipers – soon to be dubbed 'cuckoos' by the fearful Soviet soldiers – dispersed along the expected lines of attack.

The first few days went poorly for the Finns. Though they had prepared their defences well, their men were entirely untested in the face of tanks, and the appearance of large numbers of such armoured vehicles caused confusion and in some cases panic. Land, so precious to the defensive plan of Marshal Carl Gustav Mannerheim, commander-in-chief of Finland's defence forces, was in several instances given up without a fight. For the soldiers of the Red Army progress quickly came to be defined by interminable traffic jams, villages burned by the Finns to deny the Soviets their use, and unexpected dangers at every turn, as noted by Nikolai Verta in an article for *Pravda*:

> What cads! They [the Finns] can't fight and break their heads running from us, but how well they make such nastiness. They are masters of foul play … When our tired men wanted to drink, they found all the village wells filled with earth … Hardly had the first Red fighter set foot on Finnish soil when an explosion rent the air. Mines are everywhere. Moving along the Viipuri road toward the village of Jäppinen, from which the Finns had just been driven, we saw it burning, set on fire by the Finns … On every path and every road there is invisible danger prepared by a vicious and barbarious [*sic*] band. Before our eyes, mines burst under tanks, they burst under heaps of manure and hay stacks or beneath snow banks. (Quoted in Engle & Paananen 1992: 28)

For the 19th Rifle Corps making for the 'Viipuri Gateway' progress was slower than expected, in part because of stiffening resistance from the four Finnish delaying groups, but Division Commander Gorolenko's 50th Rifle Corps only had 25km to cross before it could come to grips with the Finnish main defensive line, and reached the area by 5 December. The speed of the advance on the eastern flank prompted Army Commander Kirill Afanasievich

Finnish soldiers sit in a mortar emplacement on the Taipale sector of the Mannerheim Line, 1 December 1939. In the two decades preceding the war there had not been a great deal of defensive preparation undertaken in this particular part of the Karelian Isthmus, so by the time of the Soviet invasion most of the fortifications in the area were old and barely fit for purpose. In the first flush of the Red Army's advance over the Taipale River most of the concrete bunkers were captured or destroyed, and for the remainder of the war it would be field fortifications like the one pictured that bore the brunt of Soviet attacks. (SA-kuva)

Meretskov, commander of the Leningrad Military District, to realign his forces, forming a dedicated assault force called 'Right Group', under the command of Corps Commander Vladimir Davidovich Grendal, comprising the 49th Rifle Division (Brigade Commander Pavel Ivanovich Vorobyev) and the 150th Rifle Division (Brigade Commander Sergey Alekseevich Knyazkov), together with the 19th Rifle Regiment detached from the 142nd Rifle Division. The 50th Rifle Corps, positioned to the left of 'Right Group', retained the rest of the 142nd Rifle Division as well as the 90th Rifle Division.

By bringing pressure to bear on the eastern section of the line, soon to be known as the Taipale sector, Meretskov hoped at the very least to draw off Finnish reserves from the centre and right of their line, thus making any attack there an easier proposition for the 19th Rifle Corps. If things went well and a breakthrough was achieved, the attacking rifle divisions could swing around behind the rest of the Finns' defensive line and tear at its unprotected flanks while the 10th Armoured Corps moved up and exploited the breakthrough. For such a victory they would have to cross the river line, the northern banks of which were defended by Heinrichs' III Corps: the western section was garrisoned by Colonel Claes Winell's 8th Division based around Kiviniemi, while the eastern banks up to Lake Ladoga were overseen by Colonel Viljo Kauppila's 10th Division, centred on Suvanto and Taipale. Both division commanders happened to be veterans of Jäger-Bataillon Nr. 27.

The Vuoksi River meandered eastwards, developing into Lake Suvanto which in turn became the Taipale River that gave out into Lake Ladoga. The Finns had built a line along the northern shores of these connected waterways; there were some concrete strongpoints that were relics of the 1920s, but the majority of the line was made up of earthworks, trench systems and wooden machine-gun bunkers protected by barbed wire, all of which was less than ideal.

> At Taipale … the lake makes a bend towards the south, around a spit of land forming a good bridgehead, with the Finns' line running right across the northern part of the promontory. Here at the eastern end of the Mannerheim Line foxholes and trenches were little more than drainage ditches built by farmers to keep swamp

Armas Kemppi

Armas Kemppi was born on 5 August 1893 in Hamina, a town on Finland's southern coast. Qualifying as a civil servant he took up a post with the state railway until World War I when Kemppi, like so many of the men who would define Finland's military character over the ensuing decades, joined the volunteer Jäger-Bataillon Nr. 27 in December 1915. In the Finnish Civil War he fought on the side of the White Finns, ending up as a company commander. The 1920s saw him move from post to post, completing the War College command course in 1928 before being given command of his own battalion in 1935.

On the eve of war against the Soviet Union, Kemppi was appointed commander of Infantry Regiment 30 in Colonel Viljo Kauppila's 10th Division, part of III Corps. Together with the rest of the division Kemppi's regiment moved to the Taipale sector, where they would defend

the line against the furious Soviet attacks of December 1939, remaining in position as those attacks were renewed in January 1940 and came to a crescendo the following month with Army Commander (1st rank) Semyon Konstantinovich Timoshenko's great offensive, and holding on until the final ceasefire was called on 12 March.

During the Continuation War (1941–44), Kemppi took command of Infantry Regiment 7, leading it in the Karelian battles of 1943. By 1 January 1944 he had risen to command the 20th Brigade, but this unit's poor performance in the battles around Viipuri that June saw him removed from command and gaoled for the better part of a month, suspected of dereliction of duty. Having resigned from the Finnish Army, Kemppi spent his post-military years working for the Tax Board until his death in the southern Finnish town of Sysma in 1949.

> water from flooding their fields. In many places the trenches were so narrow it was almost impossible for one man to pass another. (Engle & Paananen 1992: 67)

OPPOSITE Soviet soldiers in a trench on the Karelian Isthmus, December 1939. The experience of many Red Army men was one of shortages and hunger, Soviet logistics being unable to cope with the realities of maintaining its armies in the field in a Finnish winter. (Photo by: Sovfoto/UIG via Getty Images)

The 'promontory' of the quote was a large area of low-lying marshland called Koukkunniemi that projected southwards, hemmed in on the east and south by the Taipale River and on the west by Lake Suvanto. Rather than defend a position that was 'low, marshy, and utterly barren of cover' (Trotter 2003: 75) and which would allow them to be enfiladed from the south, west and east simultaneously, the Finns drew back to the head of the cape, turning it into 'a killing ground. Every millimeter of it had been ranged by Finnish Artillery and a fire plan worked out to bring down destruction on any force that gained a foothold there' (Trotter 2003: 76).

Grigoriy Petrovich Batsunov

Grigoriy Batsunov was born on 7 October 1917 in a small village of the Altai Mountains, near the border with Kazakhstan. His father was an NCO in Tsar Nicholas II's army, though he never returned from World War I; Grigoriy spent his childhood helping the adults in the fields during summer, and playing by the stove with his grandmother during the winter. With only a few years of education thanks to his troublemaking nature, he joined a collective farm, working mostly with horses.

Called up in 1937, Batsunov's experience with horses saw him serving in an artillery battery, and it was here that he became a good shot, eventually qualifying as a 'Voroshilov Marksman'. In 1939 his unit moved west to Byelorussia, where he was transferred to 2/756 RR in the newly formed 150th Rifle Division. The men were issued with 7.62mm SVT-38 rifles and

given training in the use of hand grenades, as well as first aid and rescuing the wounded while under fire. By the end of November 1939, the purpose of this extra training became clear as Batsunov's unit boarded a train for Karelia; moving towards the Taipale sector on the edge of Lake Ladoga, he took part in the December 1939 battles. His unit learned to respect the skill of the Finnish skiers they encountered, as well as suffering at the hands of the 'cuckoos', in one incident losing 20 men to a female sniper.

After the Winter War, Batsunov left the Red Army and married; but his respite was short, being called up again in July 1941 and joining the 426th Rifle Regiment, a unit that had veterans of the Finnish, Bessarabian and eastern campaigns among its men. Wounded twice, he survived the Great Patriotic War, dying in 1990.

MAP KEY

1   6 December: The 49th Rifle Division's 15th Rifle Regiment (Crossing 1), 222nd Rifle Regiment (Crossing 2) and 212th Rifle Regiment (Crossing 3) attack across the Taipale River, securing footholds on the Koukkunniemi promontory.

2   16–17 December: A major offensive is launched against the Finnish line by the 49th Rifle Division and the 150th Rifle Division supported by the 39th Light Tank Brigade and 240th Detached Tank Battalion (flamethrower tanks); the attack fails.

3   25 December: In the small hours of the morning, II/220 RR and the scout company of the 101st Rifle Regiment cross Lake Suvanto undetected, forming bridgeheads at Kelja, while troops from the 39th Rifle Regiment gain toeholds at Volossula and Patoniemi.

4   25 December: The Volossula and Patoniemi bridgeheads are destroyed by counter-attacks led by Captain T.A. Sorri's II/ IR 30 and Major Jaakko Sohlo's I/IR 30.

5   26–27 December: The 101st Rifle Regiment's three battalions attack across the ice one after the other in an attempt to relieve the bridgehead at Kelja, but all fail to make the far shore.

6   27 December: The Kelja bridgehead is destroyed by the concerted attacks of Captain Onni Saarelainen's 6th Detached Battalion.

Battlefield environment

Like the 'Viipuri Gateway' the Taipale sector offered opportunities for an attacking force that were lacking in the majority of the Karelian Isthmus. The land became flatter and more richly pastoral towards Lake Ladoga, with rivers and lakes that were obstacles, but surmountable ones. The eastern section of the Vuoksi waterway was made up of Lake Suvanto, which ran from Kiviniemi in a south-westerly curve down along the promontory of Koukkunniemi, at the southernmost tip of which it turned east and became the Taipale River, which in turn formed the southern and eastern flanks of Koukkunniemi before it gave out into Lake Ladoga. Koukkunniemi was low-lying with large areas of marshy ground, dotted with patches of forest; the

Finnish defensive line ran across the promontory's neck. The Finnish line had a few old concrete bunkers in the area, but these were quickly overrun or knocked out by the Soviets; the majority of the defences were simple field fortifications constructed from earth and wood, connected by a network of trenches. By the time the 'Right Group' arrived in the area at the end of the first week of December 1939, the Taipale River was still flowing, allowing for traditional river crossings to be attempted; but by the time of the final attacks on 25–27 December, the surface waters of the Taipale River and Lake Suvanto had frozen, making it possible for massed Soviet infantry formations to walk across to the Finnish side of the lake.

A view of the north shore of the Taipale River, as seen from the west. The photograph gives a good sense of the Koukkunniemi promontory's varied landscape, with low-lying ground by the river bank giving way to small hills, with a mix of trees, fields, scrub and marshland stretching out into the distance. The Taipale River ranged in width from less than 100m at its narrowest to a little over 300m at its widest point, making a crossing a difficult but achievable goal. (SA-kuva)

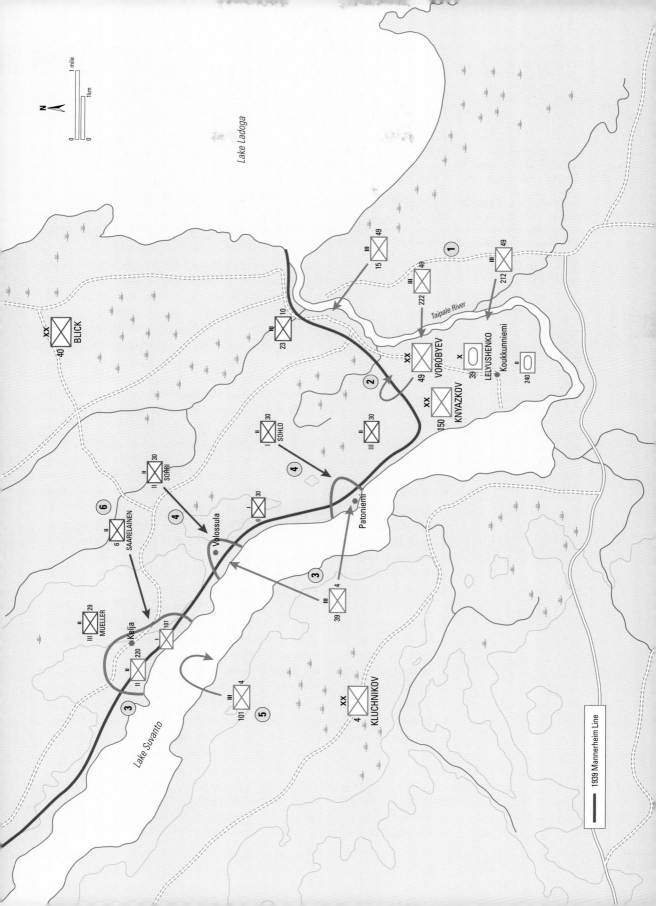

INTO COMBAT

Major-General Andrei Yegorovich Fedyunin, then a regimental officer within
the 49th Rifle Division, recalled the high spirits among the Red Army men as
they came near the Taipale River: 'The most remarkable mood affected
everyone; we were encouraged by our early successes and were eager for the
coming fight' (Fedyunin Memoir). There were a few worrying signs, such as
some shortages of food and ammunition despite the early stage of the
campaign, as well as the resistance of the four Finnish delaying groups, but
progress from the border had been relatively quick and now the immediate
prospect of attacking the Finns' main line of defence was concentrating the
minds of Soviet commanders. The route to the Taipale River was open, but
Fedyunin knew that 'forcing the crossing would be extremely difficult. It
required careful calculation as well as reconnaissance, and it would be
necessary to cover the crossings with artillery and air power; each individual
unit had to be given a fixed objective, and would need good communications
with their supporting artillery' (Fedyunin Memoir).

The first Soviet attacks across the Taipale River were conducted on
6 December by regiments of the 49th Rifle Division, followed in subsequent
days by the 150th Rifle Division; four rifle regiments (15th, 222nd, 49th and
212th) with the support of sappers and two pontoon battalions led the charge,
forcing their way across the river in the face of stiff Finnish resistance,
especially from well-directed artillery fire, at three widely dispersed sites that
were codenamed crossings 1, 2 and 3. On the receiving end was the third
battalion of Infantry Regiment 28 (III/IR 28), supported by II/IR 28, the
combined efforts of which failed to stop the Soviets from gaining limited
footholds on Koukkunniemi, reinforced that evening by a pair of rifle
regiments and a howitzer regiment. Withering Finnish machine-gun fire and
artillery barrages took a heavy toll on the attackers, but they were countered
to some degree by the efforts of the more numerous artillery batteries firing
in support of the Soviet assault. Fedyunin described how 'the whole of the
Taipale River valley from Lake Suvanto to Lake Ladoga erupted into
firestorms' (Fedyunin Memoir).

Sergeant Major V.V. Tkachev of the 19th Rifle Regiment took part in the
attack at Crossing 3, and described the action:

> The assault began. Our men ran into the field towards the river, and Finnish
> artillery immediately hit them with shrapnel. Everyone was pinned down. I was
> next to the trench at that moment. We rushed to the river along the trench. We
> reached the bank and saw the bodies of our dead sappers lying in heaps, and no
> crossing ready! The bank was steep, so we dived down to the river. There were
> several row boats below. 'Move, fellows, move!' We jumped into the boats and
> rowed like crazy, although what could we do on the other bank? Each of us had
> fifteen rifle rounds and one F-1 hand grenade. Not much of a soldier! Thirty-two
> of us made it to the other bank. (Quoted in Irincheev 2011: 14)

The Finnish artillery, so scarce in other sectors of the front, was relatively
strong in the Taipale sector; it was no match for the Red Army's guns in terms
of numbers, but great care had been taken in plotting the expected lines of
attack, resulting in Soviet assaults often being mauled as they were preparing

themselves at their jumping-off points, disrupting and dispersing many attempted crossings before they even got started. The first Soviet attempts to cross the Taipale River were all delayed by several hours for this very reason.

Holding, then expanding the bridgeheads, was the next task for the Soviets. Fedyunin anticipated Finnish counter-attacks, and he knew what to expect: 'After all, each of us, the commanders, was already well-acquainted with the tactics of the White Finns, who love to work in small groups that attack everywhere all at once' (Fedyunin Memoir). The Finns tried repeatedly – 'six rabid counterattacks' according to Fedyunin – to dislodge the Soviets. The fighting between the two sides got down to within 20–30m in some places, but the weight of Soviet fire and especially the liberal use of hand grenades helped to stem the worst of the Finnish attacks. Ammunition shortages started to loom, with at least one Soviet officer ordering his men to ready themselves for fighting with bayonets, but judicious use of limited resources meant that the Soviets managed to hold on until daybreak. The Finns, unable to eject the Soviets from Koukkunniemi, retreated to their main line across the neck of the promontory.

Limited though the successes had been, they had left the Soviet forces in a reasonable position going forward. The price, however, had been rather high, and the shock of combat, its intensity and cost, was hammered into the Red Army's soldiers. One of them, a man named Churkin from the 150th Rifle Division, made his feelings clear in a letter home:

> Sister! Starting from 6 December we have been trying to drive the enemy away and failed. I have a lot of dear friends near me, now they are no more. It was a battle. I guess you heard something about hell? The same happens here: some men cry, some complain, others shout and beg to be finished off after being wounded. The Devil himself would not understand what is going on round here. (Quoted in Irincheev 2011: 26)

Further to the west, 50th Rifle Corps' 142nd Rifle Division and 90th Rifle Division had arrived at Kiviniemi; but confusion, a lack of artillery support and poor planning led the Soviets to a hurried attempt at crossing the fast-flowing river on 7/8 December that ended in disaster, costing the 173rd Rifle Regiment scores of men missing or dead. Further attempts were made, but haste, woeful logistics and inconsistent leadership put paid to any real chance the Soviets may have had to break through at Kiviniemi. Soldiers' lives were being frittered away against objectives that never seemed to get any closer; and it became more and more difficult to force men repeatedly into the path of

A Soviet soldier surrenders near Karvia, 6 January 1940. He wears an M-36 'Kaska', the main steel helmet issued to the Red Army in the years leading up to 1939, and which saw service in the Spanish Civil War, Manchuria, Poland and finally Finland. Designed by Senior Lieutenant Aleksandr A. Shvartz (a talented officer who, one year later, would be shot in the purges for his troubles), the M-36 was notable for its prominent brim, flared sides and vent comb (designed to help ward off cavalry sabre blows). Though the example in this photograph is plain, most M-36s had a red star outline surrounding a hammer-and-sickle motif painted on the front, though as this work was carried out at the unit level rather than at the factory of production the style, size and colour of the star, hammer and sickle varied greatly. The M-36 weighed in at a reasonable 1.2kg, but it was not terribly popular with the troops due to its lack of stability and generally poor fit, though it was the overly complex and expensive production process that doomed the helmet to be replaced with the SSh-39 soon after the end of the Winter War. (SA-kuva)

the Finnish guns, as Brigade Commander P.S. Pshennikov, commander of the 142nd Rifle Division, noted: 'I remember the attack I led personally at Kiviniemi. As soon as we got under machine-gun fire, the men hit the deck and much energy was spent getting them to fulfil the task set by the army commander' (quoted in Reese 2008: 837). Such failures became permanent as the Soviet focus was drawn back to Taipale, where the initial days of fighting had borne moderate fruit. After consolidation on Koukkunniemi the Soviets had launched successive attacks on 9 and 10 December, both of which were thrown back, but their position on the promontory was secure enough for Meretskov to plan a major offensive for 15 December that would, with the 13,882-strong 49th Rifle Division and the 14,764-strong 150th Rifle Division, the supporting 39th Tank Brigade and the 240th Flamethrower Tank Battalion, break the Finnish lines wide open (Irincheev 2011: 24).

The offensive, involving all six rifle regiments in concert with scores of tanks, as well as supporting attacks at Kiviniemi and across Lake Suvanto, was a miserable failure. The Soviet artillery launched a massive bombardment, but their barrages were poorly plotted and largely ineffective, while the tank-supported infantry were quickly pinned by Finnish artillery and machine-gun

Finns manning a 76 K/02 (a Russian-made 76mm M1902 divisional gun); the Finns had 180 76 K/02s, mostly taken in 1918. Finnish artillery techniques were quite advanced, for example making use of a specially developed fire-control chart, and Waldemar Erfurth noted that 'Training and organization of the Finnish artillery is primarily designed for combat in woods and achieved a high level of efficiency during the last war, despite the fact that the armament was to some extent old-fashioned and lacked uniformity' (Erfurth 1951: 17). There were, however, significant problems. Ammunition was in desperately short supply, with the 76 K/02s starting the war with only 720 rounds apiece; and even if all went well, domestic production was expected to be able to supply barely a quarter of the 835,500 shells per month that were estimated to be needed. Combined-arms training was patchy, with breakdowns in communication between the infantry and artillery that muted the effectiveness of both. Forward observers were in short supply and were thus overworked, and on more than one occasion such men found themselves using messengers or signal flares to communicate with their artillery batteries because of a shortage of radio equipment. (SA-kuva)

fire, leaving the now unsupported Soviet tanks as ready-made targets for Finnish anti-tank guns, as recalled by a Red Army tank commander: 'The enemy pinned down our riflemen on numerous occasions in battle on 15 and 16 December, thus separating riflemen from tanks. Tanks drove forward without infantry support, crossed the anti-tank ditch and were executed by Finnish anti-tank guns while returning to own infantry at close range (100–150 metres)' (quoted in Irincheev 2011: 25). Most of those involved in the first attack never made it past the anti-tank ditch, while the supporting assaults at Kiviniemi and across Lake Suvanto came to nothing. Further attempts were made on 16 and 17 December, but they too enjoyed as little success as the first offensive. Trotter notes how the Soviet tactics were seemingly oblivious to casualties: 'One typical Russian attack during this period, lasting just under an hour, left 1,000 dead and twenty-seven burning tanks strewn on the ice' (Trotter 2003: 78).

The constant fighting and the bitter reverses took a heavy toll on the Soviet riflemen shivering in front of the Finnish lines. Rifleman Tarasov of the 150th Rifle Division expressed the misery of many:

> Father! We await death every moment … two times we were under very heavy artillery fire. Many of my comrades were killed or wounded. There were days when 600 and 700 men were killed and wounded. Trucks are evacuating the wounded day and night. By now the artillery has been firing for sixteen days, but nothing helps to drive the Finns out of there … Many men were killed here, many wounded also by friendly fire. (Quoted in Irincheev 2011: 27)

The Finns, rarely seen and seemingly indefatigable, were of course suffering as well, Rifleman Vesteri Lepistö recalling the hardships of daily existence at that stage of the war:

> Our groups were made up of seven or eight men. The pressure from lack of sleep and rest was so general that the only thought was to get out, do our jobs, and get

back as soon as possible. There was always a lack of ammunition; our hand grenades produced in seven different countries were really hazardous. Our lives were at stake every time we used them. Our most aggravating work was getting out there in forty below zero, right in front of the enemy lines to set up barbed-wire barricades. We had to work without gloves and we dared not make any noise. Everything was done at night ... I was always hungry. We couldn't eat snow because it was contaminated by grenade explosions and would cause painful stomach problems. (Quoted in Engle & Paananen 1992: 65)

Though Soviet assaults of varying strength were still made after the failures of 15–17 December, there was something of a lull while the Red Army forces regrouped for another full-blooded attempt. The old plan – attacking in full strength all along the line – was to be tried again, but this time with the addition of the 4th Rifle Division, a fresh formation that had arrived in the Taipale sector on 16 December. The division's 39th Rifle Regiment and 220th Rifle Regiment (with the 101st Rifle Regiment in reserve) would be thrown into a new assault across Lake Suvanto, hopefully surprising the Finnish 10th Division in the flank while all their other units were tied down defending against the Soviet attacks that would run all along the line from the Koukkunniemi bridgehead up to Kiviniemi. Facing the 4th Rifle Division's regiments would be the three battalions of Infantry Regiment 29 (IR 29) and one of Infantry Regiment 30 (IR 30), running in a line north-east to south-west along the shore of Lake Suvanto; Infantry Regiment 30's two remaining battalions were at Vilakkala in reserve, and the 6th Detached Battalion (the 'Hounds of Saarelainen') was also in the vicinity.

Although Lake Suvanto was a much quieter section of the front than most, it had not been entirely ignored by the Soviets. In the days leading up to the new offensive there were worrying signs that this particular stretch of shoreline was becoming more active, with Finnish scout reports of increasing Soviet activity supported by radio interceptions that indicated the Soviets were checking the thickness of the lake's ice – and yet the Finns paid no heed. Even in the face of a direct alert, as reported by signalman Lauri Keskinen of III/IR 29, there was no response: 'all hell broke loose on Christmas Day. I am still amazed – in the first hours of Christmas Day, at 2 or 4 a.m., we received a message that a Russian attack could start any time soon. The battalion commander [Captain E. Mueller] did not react to this message at all!' (quoted in Irincheev 2011: 29). At the time Captain Mueller was ignoring such warnings, the second battalion of the 220th Rifle Regiment (II/220 RR) in conjunction with a scout company of the 101st Rifle Regiment had already crossed the lake unmolested under cover of mist and falling snow, coming ashore in the area of Kelja, to be followed by the 39th Rifle Regiment which gained footholds further south at Volossula and Patoniemi just before 0700hrs on 25 December. Mueller's initial assumption was that the incursion at Kelja was most likely to have been a scouting party, and it took him all of Christmas Day and most the following night to appreciate the fact that he was dealing with a significant number of Soviet troops.

Fortunately for the 10th Division's flank, such credulous passivity did not burden other Finnish battalion commanders. Hearing reports of a Soviet incursion at Volossula, Captain T.A. Sorri led his battalion, II/IR 30, towards the lake, suffering briefly under artillery attack before his lead company began its attack at 0825hrs; a short fight ensued, with the Soviets pushed back to the lake under heavy machine-gun fire, the whole eviction taking Sorri's men a little less than an hour for a cost of eight dead and 28 wounded. The cost to the Soviets was considerably higher, Trotter noting how

> Unknowingly, the Russians had established their beachhead on a piece of terrain that was exposed to several flanking Finnish machine-gun nests, some of them only 100 meters away. When the mist evaporated, the Finnish gunners were surprised to see an unprotected swarm of enemy troops right in their sights. Eyewitness accounts of the battle state that the piles of Russian dead grew visibly larger each time the machine guns sprayed fire back and forth over the exposed landing spot. (Trotter 2003: 78)

At Patoniemi a single machine-gunner from 6th Company, I/IR 30 helped to stall the worst of the Soviet incursion, buying time for a counter-attack conducted by the rest of the battalion; the Finnish assault, led by I/IR 30's Major Jaakko Sohlo, fought throughout the day to eject the Soviets, a feat they managed by mid-evening, but at the cost of 27 wounded and 19 dead, including Major Sohlo.

For the Finns at Kelja the seriousness of their predicament was becoming clear: a sizeable Soviet force had seized a bridgehead that, if they could exploit it, would allow them to cut off the whole of the Finnish right wing, leading to the probable collapse of the entire Taipale sector. Throughout 26 December, Finnish attacks on the Soviet positions by elements of Infantry Regiment 30 and III/IR 28 were thrown back, leading to the emergency appointment of Lieutenant-Colonel Martti Nurmi to deal with the situation. Given complete control of all infantry and artillery in the area, Nurmi ordered a decisive attack by Captain Onni Saarelainen's 6th Detached Battalion for the following morning, 27 December.

At Volossula, Patoniemi and especially Kelja, Finnish machine guns and artillery pieces played a crucial role, first in taking a toll on those Red Army units that had made it across Lake Suvanto, and more importantly in disrupting every attempt made by the 4th Rifle Division to reinforce the quickly beleaguered Soviet forces. During the night of 26/27 December the Soviets launched repeated attacks across the ice, some of regimental strength, but each and every one was forced back by the Finnish artillery's interdictions – nine batteries had been committed to the fight – often with horrible casualties. The three battalions of the 101st Rifle Regiment made one such attempt, but each was cut down in turn:

> The regiment lost fifty-seven men killed and 367 men wounded. Some 318 men did make it back from the ice field and no one knew whether they were dead, alive, or taken prisoner. The regiment's commissar, Bezborodov, was wounded; the

A Politruk (political officer) reads out orders to his men on the eve of the invasion, 30 November 1939. The initial crossing of the border was marked by musical fanfares and no small amount of pomp, demonstrating that early in the war Red Army attitudes to the forthcoming war were positive, with little fear of the Finns, as noted by a soldier returning to camp after a reconnaissance mission ahead of the main Soviet lines: 'We were returning to our camp. But the first thing we saw was not our forward detachments, and not the line of infantry, but a field kitchen and a cook, stuffing snow into his pot. Someone from our group told the cook that it had been a bad idea to come so far out, that the Finns were close. "What Finns? I'll get them with my scoop." Such [an] attitude was characteristic for the majority, until we were soundly bathed in our own blood' (quoted in Reese 2011: 33). (Photo by: Sovfoto/UIG via Getty Images)

political worker of the 2nd Battalion, Vorobyev, was killed; and the commander of the 2nd Battalion, Captain Lukyanenko, was wounded. Several company commanders were lost as well. The chief of staff of the 1st Battalion did not make it back from the ice field. He carried all the commanders' codes and decoding tables with him. (Irincheev 2011: 31)

At 1030hrs on 27 December, two companies of the 6th Detached Battalion assaulted the battered Soviet bridgehead. Artillery, mortar and machine-gun support was provided, but due to a series of shortages and miscommunications the effects were muted, with the result that the initial Finnish infantry attack failed. A quick artillery barrage of the bridgehead was arranged for 1140hrs, in the midst of which a second attack went in, this time with more success, but the fight was far from over; for the next six hours the Finns and Soviets tore at each other with rifles, hand grenades and SMGs, the fight degenerating into hand-to-hand encounters, until finally the last organized Soviet resistance collapsed. Those remnants of the two Soviet units that tried to retreat across the ice were cut to pieces; most of the survivors opted to surrender instead. The 6th Detached Battalion had taken 150 casualties (49 of them killed) in the day's fighting, but the scale of the victory was clear for all to see. The frozen lake in front of the Kelja bridgehead alone was thick with Soviet dead, several thousand at least, and enough war booty was gathered up in the following days to arm a regiment of infantry.

The effect of such warfare on the average Red Army soldier was debilitating, with one infantryman from a Ukrainian battalion who had endured December's fighting on the Karelian front stating 'The whole thing is lost now … We're going to certain death. They'll kill us all. If the newspapers said that for every Finn you need ten Russkies (moskalei), they'd be right. They are swatting us like flies' (quoted in Merridale 2005: 45). The Red Army's main thrusts on the Karelian Isthmus had been surprised and bloodied in turn, their fiercest attacks thrown back, usually for little gain and great loss. In Ladoga–Karelia the 8th Army's supposed northern envelopment of the Mannerheim Line's flank had sputtered to a halt in the snows of Kollaa, while still further north the divisions of the 9th Army had by turns marched and driven into the bleak forests of central Finland, where they were fast approaching the verge of a military tragedy.

The Raate Road

23 December 1939–8 January 1940

BACKGROUND TO BATTLE

The Soviet invasion of Finland consisted of attacks along the whole Finnish line, from the Karelian Isthmus up to Petsamo in the far north. In the centre of that line some of the heaviest blows fell against the most sparsely defended Finnish positions in the country, forcing Major-General Wiljo Einar Tuompo, commander of the Northern Finland Group, to reorganize his line hastily in an attempt to counter this unexpected threat.

A Soviet supply column lies abandoned near Suomussalmi, 1 January 1940. A failure to coordinate the actions of the 163rd Rifle Division with those of the 44th Rifle Division meant that the Finns were able to deal with each force separately, thus negating the Soviet advantage in numbers. The effective destruction of the 163rd Rifle Division as a fighting force by the end of 1939 removed in large part the reason for the 44th Rifle Division's continued presence on the Raate Road; there was simply no longer any force for it to relieve. (SA-kuva)

A Finnish patrol at Suvilahti, 3 December 1939. Units of men much like those shown here fought a losing battle against the Red Army in the first days and weeks of the war, falling back in the face of overwhelming numbers of Soviet troops and vehicles. Kalevi Juntunen, a fighter with Battle Group 'Kontula' (which would later cut the Raate Road), recalled the failed attempts to stop the initial Soviet advance: 'We could only retreat in the beginning. There was very little snow on the ground and the Russian Infantry had the same mobility as us. Their tactic was like this: infantry attacked us from the front and at the same time their cavalry outflanked us through the woods. This lead unit, the 81st Mountain Rifles, was well trained. Our entire unit was around forty men – we could do little. Then we were gathered in Suomussalmi and transferred to the southern bank of Niskaselkä. The Russians captured Suomussalmi' (quoted in Irincheev 2011: 106). (SA-kuva)

The Soviet attack aimed to thunder through the Finnish countryside and seize the strategically important railway junction in the town of Oulu on the Gulf of Bothnia, which would sever Finland's only rail link with Sweden and effectively cut the country in two 'at the waist' (Trotter 2003: 143–44). This task had been given to Corps Commander Michael Pavlovich Dukhanov's 9th Army, freshly founded on 15 November 1939 only two weeks before the initial Soviet attack. The 9th Army consisted of three rifle divisions – the 44th, 122nd and 163rd – plus the 54th Mountain Rifle Division. The 122nd Rifle Division was detailed to attack Rovaniemi to the north, while the 163rd Rifle Division was tasked with taking the village of Puolanka, which lay halfway between the Soviet–Finnish border and Oulu. The 163rd Rifle Division attacked through Juntusranta in conjunction with the 81st Mountain Rifle Regiment and the 662nd Rifle Regiment, and through Raate with the 759th Rifle Regiment; the 81st Mountain Rifle and 759th Rifle regiments met at Suomussalmi (which fell on 7 December) with the aim of pressing on westward through Hyrynsalmi to Puolanka, while the 662nd Rifle Regiment turned north in an attempt to reach the town from the north-west along the Peranka–Puolanka road.

The 44th Rifle Division, commanded by Brigade Commander Alexei Ivanovich Vinogradov, was originally from the Kiev Military District, its men drawn from the flat, treeless expanse of the Ukrainian steppe. The 44th Rifle Division's rifle regiments – the 25th, 146th and 305th – together with the 122nd Artillery and 179th Howitzer regiments, the 312th Tank Battalion (from 14 December), the 56th Anti-Tank Battalion and the 3rd NKVD Regiment, began moving along the Raate Road on 12 December in support of the 163rd Rifle Division's expected advance from Suomussalmi to Puolanka.

Against this initial Soviet attack the Finns only had a smattering of border guards, home-defence units and a pair of detached battalions that could do little to stem the advance; but more Finnish troops and units were rushed to this unexpected front, the most significant of which was Colonel Hjalmar Siilasvuo's brigade-sized task force that included the poorly equipped Infantry Regiment 27 that started arriving at the Hyrynsalmi railhead on 8 December. The immediate threat posed by the 163rd Rifle Division marching on Hyrynsalmi was compounded when, on 13 December, Finnish air reconnaissance spotted the 44th Rifle Division making its way up the Raate Road. Siilasvuo realized it was imperative that he stop the 44th Rifle Division from connecting with the 163rd Rifle Division – if the two divisions could be kept apart there was a chance they could be beaten in detail; and the Finnish landscape, coupled with the rapidly deteriorating weather, would play its part in such a plan.

On 11 December, Siilasvuo launched the first of his counter-attacks, an unending series of which would run until 28 December, including an assault on the Raate Road, cutting it and forming a roadblock on the river that crossed the 1.5km-wide gap between Lake Kuivasjärvi and Lake Kuomajärvi (a little over 9km south-east of Suomussalmi). This roadblock saw no sign of the Soviets for several days, the advance of the 44th Rifle Division having been slowed as much by its own logistical problems as by Finnish action, allowing Siilasvuo to focus his full attention on the 163rd Rifle Division. In theory, the two Soviet regiments defending the village were more than strong enough to deal with the scrappy Finnish forces that stood in their way, but several factors were counting against them. The 81st Mountain Rifle Regiment had fought hard to get to where it was, but no supplies or new drafts of men had been forthcoming. There was little contact and almost no cooperation between the 81st and the 759th Rifle Regiment, both regiments making little use of their superiority in artillery and relying instead on their infantry, while their supporting armour was mostly still at Juntusranta, marooned due to lack of fuel.

During 13–16 December, Siilasvuo launched a counter-attack against the 163rd Rifle Division and, to a lesser extent, against the 44th Rifle Division, supported by a series of harrying raids designed to knock the Soviets off balance and deny them any chance of retaking the initiative. The Finnish military writer Colonel J.A. Järvinen described the process thus:

> Usually before an operation, the patient receives an anesthetic so that he will not suffer unduly during the surgery, or kick too much. So before the operation began [in which the Finns were fighting the 163d] small local anesthetics were applied [to the 44th], the purpose of which was not to alleviate suffering but to prevent the patient from kicking. In order to numb the long, huge Russian snake, numerous small encircling operations were applied alongside its body. (Quoted in Engle & Paananen 1992: 96)

Finnish reinforcements continued to arrive (eventually becoming the 9th Division), helping Siilasvuo to maintain the pressure on the harried Soviets.

The seemingly endless Finnish counter-attacks threw the Red Army regiments positioned around Suomussalmi onto the defensive. The commander of the 163rd Rifle Division, Brigade Commander Andrei Ivanovich Zelentsov, was under significant pressure and asked Corps Commander Dukhanov for permission to withdraw, but Dukhanov refused, citing as his reason the expected arrival of the relieving force of the 44th Rifle Division. Irincheev notes that despite such assurances, Dukhanov 'failed to arrange a coordinated operation by the divisions' (Irincheev 2011: 107–08), a situation hardly improved by Dukhanov's replacement on 22 December by Corps Commander Vasily Ivanovich Chuikov. The paralysing slowness of the Soviet response to the attacks on Suomussalmi, exemplified by the inability of the 44th Rifle Division to mount any sort of effective breakthrough even though it was facing weaker units and was a scant 9km from the positions of the 163rd Rifle Division, proved to be disastrous when Siilasvuo launched another attack on 27 December. The lines of the 163rd Rifle Division broke, forcing a general retreat across Lake Kiantojärvi, effectively abandoning the 662nd Rifle Regiment to annihilation by the harrying Finns. Siilasvuo now turned his full attention to the Raate Road and to the 44th Rifle Division strung out along its length.

A Finnish soldier examines a Soviet sniping rifle, most likely captured in one of the battles around Suomussalmi and the Raate Road, 13 February 1940. The rifle, a 7.62mm Mosin-Nagant M1891-30 with a 4.2×29 PEM telescopic sight and mount (dating its production to the years 1936–38), would have been manufactured in the armaments factories of Tula and Izhevsk. Selections were taken from the production line, refined (with particular attention paid to the trigger assembly), then tested for accuracy. A Red Army sniper would be expected to hit a target at 400m with open sights, increasing to 800m with telescopic sights. Though Soviet sniper doctrine was well established by 1939, their impact on the course of the Winter War was rather muted, the laurels going to their similarly armed Finnish counterparts. Though, as with almost everything else, the Finnish Army was desperately short of sniping rifles, captured weapons like the one shown here were usually kept by the individuals who took them, to be used as personal hunting rifles when they returned to civilian life. (SA-kuva)

MAP KEY

1   23–28 December: Captain Simo Mäkinen reinforces the roadblock put up by the Finnish Battle Group 'Kontula' between lakes Kuomajärvi and Kuivasjärvi, which on 11 December had cut the Raate Road before Brigade Commander Alexei Ivanovich Vinogradov's 44th Rifle Division could come to the aid of the 163rd Rifle Division at Suomussalmi. Mäkinen's force fends off Soviet assaults while launching spoiling attacks of its own against the 25th Rifle Regiment, stopping the 44th Rifle Division from making any progress.

2   27–30 December: The 163rd Rifle Division is forced out of its positions in Suomussalmi and retreats in disarray to the Soviet–Finnish border.

3   1–2 January: Captain Eino Lassila's I/IR 27 and Sissi P-1 attack Soviet positions on the Raate Road near Haukila, beginning the process of cutting up the Soviet line into *motti* segments. On 2 January, Captain Aarne Airimos' III/IR 27 attacks Captain Pastukhov's II/146 RR on Lassila's left near Haukila Farm.

4   2–4 January: Task Force Kari attacks towards the Kokkojärvi road junction, while Lieutenant-Colonel Frans Fagernäs manoeuvres II/IR 64 and III/IR 64 into position in readiness for the final attack.

5   5 January: Colonel Hjalmar Siilasvuo launches a general attack on the 44th Rifle Division with all four task forces (Mandelin, Mäkiniemi, Kari and Fagernäs), overrunning the headquarters of both the 25th Rifle Regiment and the 146th Rifle Regiment. Task Force Fagernäs cuts the bridge at Purasjoki.

6   6 January: Soviet positions begin to collapse. Vinogradov orders a breakout for 2200hrs, with one group (Vinogradov's 44th Rifle Division) moving through the forest, while the other (Major Plyukhin's 25th Rifle Regiment) moves along the road. Plyukhin's column is destroyed; Vinogradov's escapes. The final pockets of remaining Soviet resistance are crushed by 8 January.

Battlefield environment

Langdon-Davies observed that 'Finland consists entirely of natural obstacles. Unlike most other countries, it does not merely have difficult boundaries enclosing a vulnerable interior. Every acre of its surface was created to be the despair of an attacking military force' (Langdon-Davies 1941: 7). Such a description could certainly apply to the Raate Road, a narrow unmetalled roadway that stretched from the Soviet–Finnish border to the village of Suomussalmi. The forest – *the* defining feature of the Finnish landscape – encroached on the road for most of its length, with the treeline sometimes starting on the verge, and other times within 20–30m of scrubland that flanked the narrow course. Generally the road was too narrow to allow units and vehicles to pass one another with anything other than great

difficulty. Passage through the trees was out of the question; the density of the forest coupled with the snow made an impassable barrier for vehicles, and an intimidatingly unfamiliar environment for Soviet troops more used to the open steppe. Trying to move through the snow without skis was slow and very tiring, and those Red Army men who did have skis were not properly trained in their use. Lakes and waterways dotted the landscape; once they froze they were of great use to the Finnish defenders, who constructed ice roads on their surfaces, allowing them to move along the flanks of the Soviet positions – sometimes only a few kilometres from the road – with speed and efficiency, entirely unobserved by the Soviet column.

Finnish troops march along the Raate Road in the summer of 1941. The photograph gives a clear sense of how narrow and unsuitable such a passage was for an armoured column of moderate size, let alone that of a full division with supporting elements – around 17,000 men, hundreds of vehicles and thousands of horses. Note how the forest quickly swallows the flanks of the road towards the top of the picture; the majority of the 20km of road occupied by the 44th Rifle Division would have looked like this, blanketed in snow. (SA-kuva)

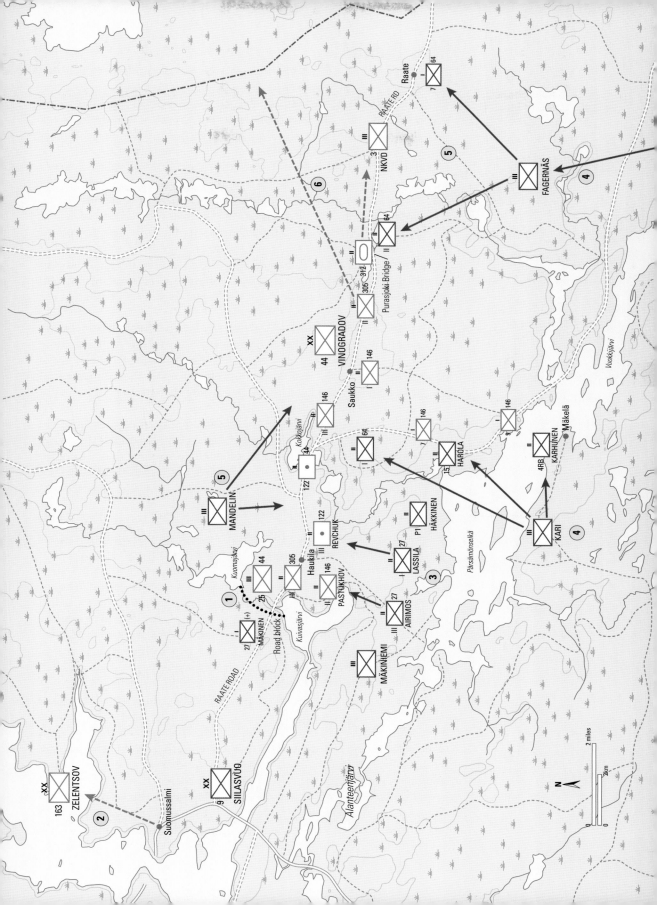

INTO COMBAT

The growing presence of the 44th Rifle Division on his south-eastern flank had been a constant worry for Siilasvuo; his instinct to cut the Raate Road on 11 December had presaged the arrival of the Soviet division, and would prove to be a sound decision. Initially secured by Battle Group 'Kontula', the roadblock was quickly reinforced with two companies from Infantry Regiment 27 under Captain Simo Mäkinen. On 15 December the leading unit of the 44th Rifle Division, the 25th Rifle Regiment, launched an attack on the roadblock with a company battlegroup which was repulsed, leading to an unaccountable period of inactivity from Vinogradov's force, which undertook no offensive manoeuvres for a week despite the increasing pressure being applied to the besieged men of the 163rd Rifle Division only a few kilometres to the north-west. A captured Soviet regimental commander spoke of the Soviet view of trying to break through the Finnish line: 'Of course we tried to attack and open the road forward, but it was like hitting your head against a wall. It was different from what we were used to in our previous battles, in Poland, for instance. It was unbelievable' (quoted in Engle & Paananen 1992: 103).

On 23 December Captain Mäkinen took the initiative, launching a surprise attack on the head and flanks of the 25th Rifle Regiment from Haukila and in the area of Lake Kokkojärvi. The raid caused a fair degree of damage but the more significant impact was upon the confidence of Vinogradov and his commanders, among whom the attacks had 'created so much confusion and fear that the 44th Division never recovered its balance' (Chew 2007: 99). Constant raids, coming at any time of day or night right along the length of the road, disoriented the Soviets, who found themselves unable to hit back at attackers who arrived with no warning, caused mayhem and then vanished before any organized counter-attack could be put together.

The long, slow advance of the 44th Rifle Division was expected and followed closely by the Finns, whose use of mobile intercept detachments that operated in direct support of field commanders produced excellent results in the compromising of Red Army radio communications, with one officer near Suomussalmi, Captain Marttinen, usually receiving 'decoded and translated copies of enemy messages within 4 to 5 hours of their transmission … In some cases, such messages were read within 2 hours' (Chew 2007: 276). In addition to such communications intercepts, Colonel Siilasvuo had a single reconnaissance aircraft which was effective mostly due to the Soviet practice of sticking almost entirely to the roads, making them straightforward to locate. Finally, the increasing patrols of Finnish scouts, gliding silently through the forests and rarely spotted by their enemies, completed the intelligence picture.

In contrast, the Soviet view of the surroundings into which they were moving ever deeper became increasingly confused and bleak. Matters were made worse for the Soviet patrols thanks to the absence of any parallel roads to allow for reconnaissance screens, thus forcing such patrols to slog through the dense snow little more than several hundred metres either side of the main column on the road. As the division continued on its journey, such outlying patrols would come under sudden and terrifying attacks that would cease and disappear just as quickly as they had started; the natural effect of such assaults was to force the Red Army reconnaissance screens back towards the road, reducing their usefulness to the point where they could offer no real warning of Finnish movements or attacks.

Further Finnish preparation had been undertaken in the form of an ice road constructed across a series of connected lakes – Alanteenjärvi, Pärsämönselkä and Vuokkijärvi – which ran in a more or less parallel line around 8km to the south of the Raate Road. The ice road allowed quick movement of Finnish forces and supplies along the length of their southern axis of attack; such a facility allowed not only rapid

A knocked-out T-26 light infantry tank lies frozen in the snow on the Raate Road, 8 January 1940. Such vehicles proved to be tactically unsuitable to the terrain of central Finland, with many running out of fuel and ending up as impromptu defensive emplacements dotted up and down the Soviet lines. The Soviet tank force was in a state of flux, the tank corps having been disbanded just prior to the Winter War. According to the November 1939 reorganization, a light-tank brigade (*c.*2,896 men with 162 T-26s) had a reconnaissance battalion (one armoured-car company with 16 armoured cars, one motorized rifle company and one light-tank company with 16 T-37 light tanks), three tank battalions (267 men each, with 54 T-26s), a motorized-rifle battalion (669 men) and various support elements. A heavy-tank brigade (*c.*2,318 men with 92 T-28 medium tanks) was made up of a reconnaissance company (ten BA-20 armoured cars and six BT light tanks), three tank battalions (335 men each with ten T-28s, five BA-20s and three BTs) and various support units. (SA-kuva)

redeployment in support of attacks or withdrawals, but also acted as a force multiplier – at least in the eyes of the enemy – as the relatively small Finnish detachments that struck the Soviet line in multiple places over a short period of time added to the Soviet commander Vinogradov's sense that he was surrounded by increasingly large Finnish formations. Winter roads were also constructed – a labour-intensive process involving the compacting snow with horses and sledges of increasing weight until a hard-packed 'road' was created – running from key points such as supply hubs or jumping-off points up to the ice road as well as towards the Raate Road itself.

By the time of Captain Mäkinen's attacks on 23 December, the vast majority of the 44th Rifle Division was spread out along almost 32km of the Raate Road, from the border to the roadblock. Repeated plans to break through the roadblock and come to the relief of the 163rd Rifle Division went awry, were postponed or were spoiled by Finnish actions, so that by the time the 163rd had been routed all pretence at advancing had been done away with and the 44th Rifle Division was ordered to dig in and defend the road. The 44th was well supplied with vehicles, guns and tanks, but the narrow road and the impassability of the terrain either side of it meant that the impact of the division's firepower and mobility was dramatically weakened, basically reducing its effectiveness to the area of the road on which it was stuck, intermixed with groups of infantry that had dug in along the length of the road in platoon-, company- and battalion-sized pockets.

Owing to steady reinforcement during the previous week, Siilasvuo now had a decent balance of forces at his disposal. Justifiably elated by their recent victory, these forces enabled Siilasvuo to put his plan for the 44th Rifle Division into action. Four new task forces were formed from the 9th Division, each named for its commander: Lieutenant-Colonel Karl Mandelin (Infantry Regiment 65); Colonel Johan Mäkiniemi (Infantry Regiment 27); Major Kaarle Kari (I/IR 64), and Lieutenant-Colonel Frans Fagernäs (II/IR 64 and III/IR 64). In addition, there was an independent light-infantry battalion commanded by Captain Ahti Paavola, the 15th Detached Battalion led by Captain Harola, Lieutenant Karhunen's 4th Replacement Battalion and

Captain Häkkinen's 1st *Sissi* Battalion 'P-1' ('*Sissi*' literally means 'guerrilla', though they were in effect light infantry rather than partisans). Despite the fact that the 9th Division was a brand-new entity, all four task-force commanders had served with Siilasvuo in the Finnish volunteer Jäger-Bataillon Nr. 27 in the Imperial German Army during World War I, and so trusted one another and were well used to working together. Mandelin's force was to take up position to the north of the Raate Road by Lake Kuomajärvi, while Mäkiniemi, Kari and Fagernäs were to position their forces along the southern flank of the road, at Kuivasjärvi, Mäkelä and Heikkilä respectively.

The Finnish plan called for the encirclement of the Soviet position, with repeated attacks breaking up that line into smaller, more easily manageable sections by means of *motti* tactics. The road-cutting exercise was usually conducted in a well-practised manner: the chosen unit would approach the target by stealth along pre-determined routes, carrying only weapons, explosives and camouflage; a brief but intense burst of mortar and machine-gun fire would then follow to saturate the target area which would then be assaulted by infantry, causing as much havoc as possible.

> The main purpose of the raid was not to wipe out every Russian Soldier along a given piece of the Raate Road. It was to sever the column by overwhelming localised impact and knife through to the woods on the other side. Once a breach had been torn in the Soviet column, no matter how narrow, fresh reserves would swarm out of the forest to consolidate and widen the gap, including combat engineers who would immediately, under fire, start fortifying the sides of the original breach. Eventually … each road-cut was 300 to 440 meters wide, with strong barricades and earthworks sealing it off at both ends. (Trotter 2003: 156)

The first blow fell on the night of 1/2 January 1940 when Captain Eino Lassila, commander of I/IR 27, led his battalion together with *Sissi* P-1 against the strongest part of the Soviet line near the head of the road, which was defended by two battalions of the 25th Rifle Regiment and two battalions of the 146th Rifle Regiment (II/146 RR under Captain Pastukhov was stationed by Lake Kuivasjärvi) as well as by a significant number of tanks and artillery pieces. Lassila's force travelled along a winter road that looped around the southern end of Lake Kuivasjärvi, and after a brief pause at 1700hrs to rest and have a hot meal, moved through the silent darkness on skis, their heavy weapons and ammunition carried on *ahkio* sledges. Arriving at a ridge that stood 365m from the road, Lassila's force noted that the Red Army men were clearly visible, huddled around numerous fires scattered along the road. Lassila sent two companies towards the road side by side, one to sweep left and the other right, each supported by half-a-dozen Maxim machine guns set up along the ridge, with the third company in reserve.

By a happy accident of poor navigation the Finnish companies were 450m off the mark and instead of approaching a thickly defended section of the Soviet line at Haukila Farm, they were instead about to encounter the third battalion of the 122nd Artillery Regiment (III/122 AR) under the command of Captain Revchuk. Exhausted after a long march, Revchuk's artillerymen of the 7th and 8th batteries had set the guns in their firing positions – aiming east – but had not made them ready to fire, having decided to leave that chore

A section of the Raate Road, showing the carnage and destruction the Finns inflicted on the Soviet units trapped there. The commander of the 44th Rifle Division, Brigade Commander Alexei Ivanovich Vinogradov, made a desperate call to his superiors on 5 January, the day of Siilasvuo's all-out attack, begging for help: 'the situation of the division is hard, especially with food, men are exhausted and starved, we have about 400 wounded, horses are dying, no petrol, most of the horses are killed, we are almost out of ammo. Enemy is attacking us from the front … morale is low, some commanders are deserting from the battlefield, I request urgent help' (44th Rifle Division War Diary). The 9th Army did not have much in the way of help to give, however, and even if it had, the collapse had already begun. By the following evening the last cohesive units were breaking out as and when they could, streaming though the forests back to the Soviet border. (SA-kuva)

for the morning; the 9th Battery personnel were still standing by the road. Lassila's men overwhelmed the spare sentry line 55m out from the road, and advanced through the darkness to the edge of the Soviet position just as the mortars and Maxims opened fire. The 9th Battery was annihilated almost immediately; the 7th and 8th batteries did not fare much better, eventually being driven from their guns, the survivors joining the 146th Rifle Regiment. The road was cut, with trees felled and mined to make barricades at either end of the breach. A desperate Soviet counter-attack was launched, led by an armoured car company and various infantry elements, but the Finns, in expectation of such a move, had brought up a pair of precious 37mm Bofors anti-tank guns in support; they caused havoc among the armoured cars, dispatching at least seven of them.

A similar attack by Captain Aarne Airimos' III/IR 27 against Pastukhov's II/146 RR on Lassila's left caused hundreds of Soviet casualties, but was fought off with the help of I/146 RR. All along the line Finnish patrols were striking, causing destruction at every opportunity. Field kitchens, large, ponderous and easily spotted, were a prime target, as were officers who were picked off by well-hidden snipers. Attempts by groups of Red Army men to shelter by large fires led to mortar attacks and sniper fire, leaving them in the invidious position of having to choose between being shelled or frozen. The Soviet regimental commander from the 44th Rifle Division recalled how deadly such times had become:

> But Finns we couldn't see anywhere. And believe it or not, the first Finns that I personally saw were the two that took me as a prisoner after my regiment was destroyed. We couldn't see them anywhere, yet they were all over the place. If anybody left the campsite, he met with certain death. When we sent our sentries to take their positions around the camp, we knew that within minutes they would be dead with a bullet hole in the forehead or the throat slashed by a dagger. This invisible death was lurking from every direction. It was sheer madness. Hundreds, even thousands of my men were slaughtered. (Quoted in Engle & Paananen 1992: 103)

Last stand on the Raate Road

By the evening of 5 January 1940 the Soviet positions on the Raate Road had begun to unravel. Once the 163rd Rifle Division had been defeated, Colonel Hjalmar Siilasvuo turned the full force of the 9th Division on the 44th Rifle Division; through a series of attacks all along the southern flank of the Soviet positions on the Raate Road the Finns cut Vinogradov's force into a number of isolated pieces – 'islands' of men, guns and vehicles – that were unable to support one another. Harried and worn down by hit-and-run attacks, the Soviet enclaves were denied food and warmth as their field kitchens and fires were the prime targets of snipers and mortars; vehicles were mostly out of fuel with tanks serving as immobile gun positions, while the 'Condition of horses that have not received hay for 5–7 days in the cold conditions is really bad' (44th Rifle Division War Diary). Vinogradov reported how the 'enemy is concentrating forces in order to cut the defenses of the division. Due to lack of food morale is extremely low, horses are dying, petrol and ammo are almost spent' (44th Rifle Division War Diary). The headquarters of the 146th Rifle Regiment, commanded by Major Ievliev, was near the head of the Soviet positions on the Raate Road, far from any sort of help. The position was dire, with most of Ievliev's regiment's units spread out in unsupported outposts that, one by one, started to fall silent. Friday 5 January saw a major offensive by the Finns that finally started to break the Red Army defences apart, with the headquarters of the 25th Rifle Regiment overwhelmed, followed by similar attacks on the 146th Rifle Regiment's headquarters. Ievliev, wounded in earlier fighting, sent a desperate message at 1945hrs on 5 January stating how 'the 146th regiment suffered heavy losses, we have very little power left, I need help' (44th Rifle Division War Diary). Later that same night, Ievliev sent his last communication from the surrounded 146th Rifle Regiment headquarters, uncoded and repeated several times: 'Give us help, they are finishing us off, give us help' (44th Rifle Division War Diary).

Despite the dire shortages of food and ammunition, negligible help for the wounded, and the terrible biting cold for which they were so ill-prepared, the Soviet troops did not simply sit and await their fate; nor, by and large, did they surrender – they fought. The performance of the senior commanders was, for the most part, lamentable; they were unable to organize effective defensive postures or to coordinate in even the most rudimentary way with other groups in the same situation to their mutual benefit. The soldiers, however, kept fighting, sometimes to the bitter end. Every Finnish attack was met with stiff resistance, and localized counter-attacks, though usually doomed due to their disparate and uncoordinated nature, were thrown against each new incursion.

In the meantime, to the south-east, Major Kari's force launched attacks that put it within 3.5km of the Kokkojärvi road fork by 4 January, while Fagernäs' two battalions used the same time to manoeuvre to within easy striking distance of the road in anticipation of the final blow. Siilasvuo gave orders for a concerted all-out attack from both north and south of the road on the following day, 5 January; but despite the desperate state of the Soviet defenders and the zeal with which the Finns pressed home their assaults, a decisive breakthrough still failed to materialize, though Fagernäs' group did manage to cut the bridge at Purasjoki as well as the last stage of the road less than 2km from the border, denying the remnants of the 44th Rifle Division any clear route of escape. The fighting all along the line was intense, with Lassila's I/IR 27 still holding the same stretch of road that it had captured three days earlier, losing 96 men in the face of desperate Soviet attempts to break out of their grim fastness. Lassila's request to pull back was angrily refused, with the stinging injunction that no one else was any better off than he, and that his choices were to stay and fight or retreat and be shot.

There was to be no respite. The Finnish attacks of 5 January had been furiously repulsed, but Siilasvuo pressed home again the next day, and the

A Finnish reindeer patrol making the most of its *ahkio* sledges near Jäniskoski, 20 February 1940. Lieutenant Dmitrii Krutskikh of the 54th Mountain Rifle Division envied the simplicity and effectiveness of the Finnish *ahkios*: 'The Finns also had those little sleds (ahkios) which could carry a machine gun, ammunition or the wounded. They were light, lined with thin metal sheets underneath. These sleds glided in the snow like on water! The ahkio had two straps – a long one and a shorter one – to be pulled by two men. We did not have anything like that. Say, somebody gets wounded on a recon mission (and I did have such misfortunes), how [to] carry him back twenty–thirty kilometres in that terrain? Impossible! We make a hundred metres – everybody can barely breathe! Of course, we tried to make some sort of stretchers. But was it ever hard to carry people on them! When we took Finnish ahkios – we weren't allowed to use them. Later on, we began building our own, with wooden box planks, but ours were triangular, with sidings on the edges' (Krutskikh Interview). (SA-kuva)

Soviet positions, pushed far beyond their breaking point, began to come apart. As the previous day had begun to wane the headquarters of the 25th Rifle Regiment had been overrun. The headquarters of the 146th Rifle Regiment also were attacked, the wounded commander Major Ievliev sending a last desperate uncoded radio message: 'Give us help, they are finishing us off, give us help' (44th Rifle Division War Diary); the message was repeated several times, then fell silent. By mid-afternoon on 6 January it was clear that the Soviet positions were starting to collapse, so Vinogradov decided to break out later that day at 2200hrs. He organized two columns, the first of which – led by Major Plyukhin of the 25th Rifle Regiment – would try to break through the Raate Road while a second column commanded by Vinogradov himself would strike out into the woods. When the time came Vinogradov's column reached Soviet lines without incident, but Plyukhin's road column was torn to pieces almost as soon as it started to move.

The collapse of the remains of the 44th Rifle Division happened in a piecemeal way, with pockets of resistance fighting on until 8 January. A few units kept some semblance of cohesion and made it back to their own lines, but most disintegrated, with men making their own way out of the icy nightmare as best they could, or falling prisoner to the Finns in the process. For Vinogradov escape was only temporary, however. With such a disaster there had to be someone to blame, and as Vinogradov had the bad grace to

Corps Commander Vasily Ivanovich Chuikov's chief of staff, D.N. Nikishev, noted that 'Our units, saturated by technology (especially artillery and transport vehicles), are incapable of manoeuvre and combat in this theatre: they are burdened and chained down by technology which can only go by road … combat in special conditions is not studied – they [the troops] are frightened by the forest and cannot ski' (quoted in Van Dyke 1997: 88). Here, Finnish fighters pose around a captured T-28 tank, taken near Summa in December 1939. Though the Red Army deployed various heavy and experimental tanks in the field, by far and away the most numerous and effective was the T-28. It weighed 28 tonnes (32 tonnes with appliqué armour), had a crew of six and was armed with a 76.2mm main gun and four 7.62mm machine-guns (two of them mounted on smaller turrets). It was a difficult beast to deal with, as it tended to be far more resistant to Molotov cocktails than its smaller brother, the T-26; the Finns' newly acquired 37mm Bofors anti-tank guns could penetrate the T-28's 30mm frontal armour, but the Soviets quickly upgraded that to 80mm before Timoshenko's big push in 1940, making it much more formidable. (SA-kuva)

escape with his life he was a natural candidate for court martial, along with his staff. Found guilty on 11 January – less than a week after he had slipped past the Finns – Vinogradov was executed by firing squad, along with the division's Commissar I.T. Parkhomenko and its chief of staff Colonel Onurfi I. Volkov, the official reason being his loss of the 44th Rifle Division's entire stock of field kitchens. There seems little doubt that Vinogradov was not up to the task of leading a division; his hesitancy, absence of boldness and any shred of initiative, must blacken his reputation to some degree. That being said, he was in a position that better men than he would have found trying in the extreme, added to which he received negligible support from his corps and army commanders, who offered him no help in trying to either sustain his position or retreat in good order.

Finland's victories at Suomussalmi and the Raate Road were immediately cast in the most spectacular terms, with the international press invited to marvel at the horror of destruction that the Finns, easily cast in the role of plucky underdogs, had dealt out to their intemperate aggressor. The Finns' tally of captured arms and equipment was impressive. The 44th Rifle Division lost all its heavy equipment, including all its field kitchens, together with 4,822 rifles, 190 light machine guns, 106 heavy machine guns, 29 anti-tank guns, 14 anti-aircraft trucks with quad-mounted Maxims, 71 field and anti-aircraft guns, 43 tanks, ten armoured cars, 260 trucks, two cars and 1,170 horses (Irincheev 2011: 115). The more significant spoils included modern communications equipment, especially prized due to its relative rarity in the Finnish armed forces. Casualties for the Finns for the whole Suomussalmi–Raate campaign were estimated at 2,700 men; Soviet losses were put at between 22,500 and 27,000, though Irincheev thinks the real number is somewhat lower, with the 44th Rifle Division suffering 4,674 casualties – 1,001 killed, 1,430 wounded, and 2,243 missing in action (Irincheev 2011: 115). Whatever the true figure, the enormity of the Soviet defeat in central Finland would not be measured by statistics alone.

'Millionaire' and 'Poppius' Bunkers

11–13 February 1940

BACKGROUND TO BATTLE

The war had not gone well anywhere for the Soviets except for where it mattered least – in arctic Petsamo, far away in the frozen mists of the north; everywhere else the Red Army had been thwarted, bloodied and beaten in battle after battle. The initial intention had been to cross the Mannerheim Line in little more than a week, with Viipuri falling shortly afterwards, leading to a victory parade in Helsinki on 21 December, Stalin's birthday, but the 7th, 8th and 14th armies had singularly failed to make any appreciable dent in the Finnish defences. The new year started with stalemate on the Karelian Isthmus and Ladoga–Karelia, with the disaster of Suomussalmi fast being compounded by the imminent collapse of the 44th Rifle Division on the Raate Road, hammering a nail through the heart of any hope of success in northern Finland. Setbacks such as these were impossible for Stalin and Stavka to ignore, and so a series of radical changes were initiated as the year turned.

The new seriousness began with the renaming of the theatre of operations as the North-Western Front, with Army Commander (1st rank) Semyon Konstantinovich Timoshenko given command and Corps Commander Georgy Zhukov as his chief of staff; Timoshenko was no new Alexander, but he was competent, professional and ideologically sound. Most importantly, Stalin agreed to give him the resources and time that he needed to prepare his offensive against the Finns – gifts his predecessors had not enjoyed. The North-Western

A Finnish anti-tank team with their Swedish-made Bofors 37 PstK/36 in position on Ruhtinaanmäki, 14 January 1940. The 37mm Bofors anti-tank gun proved crucial to the Finnish defensive strategy of the war, and quickly showed itself capable of handling all types of Soviet tanks (apart from the rare KV-1 heavy tank). The Finns had only managed to secure 48 of these guns by the time war broke out; another 66 were imported from Sweden as the war progressed, but the overall shortage became critical when the enormous number of tanks committed to the invasion by the Red Army became apparent. Finnish anti-tank teams quickly got into the habit of firing the gun and then immediately moving it to another prepared position, firing quickly, then moving once again. The Bofors anti-tank guns were also installed in the larger bunkers that made up the Mannerheim Line, but they were too few in number and spread so thinly that the loss of a single gun or its crew (as at 'Poppius' bunker) allowed Soviet tanks to range freely right up to the gun-ports of the bunkers in the overwhelming assaults of 11 February 1940. (SA-kuva)

Front was reorganized, with Grendal's 'Right Group' evolving into the 13th Army and retaining its responsibility for the Taipale sector, while the 7th Army, concentrated on the western flank of the Isthmus, was given to a demoted Meretskov, replacing the dismal Army Commander (2nd rank) Vsevolod Fedorovich Yakovlev who had been sent packing to Leningrad in disgrace.

Timoshenko spent January 1940 building up overwhelming numbers of men, tanks and guns; 23 rifle divisions (14 of them in the 7th Army, nine in the 13th Army) were supported by five tank brigades, 15 air regiments and 2,800 artillery pieces in the 76–280mm range, enough for 50 guns per kilometre of front. The divisions that would lead the assault rehearsed their attacks, carefully planning how they would take their objectives, and were also given extra training to improve their hitherto lacklustre tactical performance. New life and purpose seemed to be taking hold. The historian Allen Chew notes how the morale of the average Red Army man was changing during this period:

> According to Soviet sources, the Red Army launched the February offensive amid enthusiastic shouts, 'To the attack for the glory of the Fatherland!' There is no question that nationalistic appeals struck a more responsive chord with the Russian soldier than did the alleged glories of socialism. There was a subtle and gradual change in the mood of some of the survivors of the December battles. Soloviev, a veteran of the Isthmus fighting … described this mood as a widespread feeling of humiliation. Although not hating the Finns, some of those Russians felt that the 'insult' – the shadow cast on Russia's reputation – had to be avenged; the Finns had to be beaten. Thus a sense of shame and degradation was being transformed into a fighting spirit. (Chew 2007: 138)

Timoshenko's new plan for the Karelian Isthmus was blunt and realistic: batter the defenders into insensibility with constant probing attacks all along the line and round-the-clock artillery bombardments, followed by a massive front-wide offensive led by an armoured 'hammer' that would punch through the Mannerheim Line, opening a breach that succeeding waves of men and machines would keep open. Much of Karelia was laced with lakes, rivers, swamps and forests, but the 16km-wide 'Viipuri Gateway', centred on the villages of Summa and Lähde, offered a broadly flat expanse of sparsely wooded land unobstructed by excessive natural obstacles; this was where Timoshenko's main attack would fall.

Such a potentially troublesome gap was well defended by the Finns, who concentrated significant resources on the fortification of the area: a network of 35 concrete bunkers armed with Maxim machine guns and 37mm Bofors anti-tank guns (on the rare occasions that any of the latter were to be had) was supplemented with trench complexes, wooden bunkers, barbed-wire entanglements, anti-tank ditches and obstacles (usually constructed from granite boulders), wooden barricades, minefields and deliberately flooded ground. The nature of the Finnish defences is well-described by Irincheev:

The sectors of fire of the bunkers were placed so that the bunkers could lay down flanking fire on the lines of barbed wire and anti-tank barrier obstacles. Bunkers often had interlocking sectors of fire. Enemy armour was supposed to be stopped by the obstacles before being dealt with by the anti-tank artillery and close-range weapons of the Finnish infantry. The Finnish officers were well aware of the weakness of their anti-tank artillery, but at the same time they knew that armour alone would not be able to control the captured terrain. Thus, the Finnish defenders of the Line saw their main task as isolating the Soviet armour from the advancing infantry and then dealing with them separately. The Finnish troops on the isthmus were issued strict orders to hold their ground and fight, even if they found themselves surrounded by the enemy. (Irincheev 2013: 23)

A 203mm M1931 (B-4) heavy howitzer, one of the largest corps-level artillery pieces available to the Red Army. Such heavy pieces, as well as the monstrous 280mm M1939 (Br-5) mortar, were so big they required an integral tracked carriage to enable them to move. They were the ultimate expression of the Soviet belief in the power of artillery to dominate the battlefield. The super-heavy artillery battalions were parcelled out, one per rifle division, where they would add their reach to the hundreds of artillery guns of every calibre that were assembled for Timoshenko's big push. The attacks of 1 February and then 11 February 1940 provided ample opportunity for the Soviet artillerymen to prove the worth of their weapons. (Courtesy of the Central Museum of the Armed Forces, Moscow via Stavka)

This would not be the first fight of the war for the Finns guarding the Viipuri Gateway. On 17 December 1939, as the major offensive in the Taipale sector was falling apart, the left flank of the 7th Army had launched concerted attacks on Summa and the nearby Lähde road in an attempt to force a path through the Mannerheim Line, battering the defenders in a series of tank and infantry assaults over a period of five days. The fighting cost the Soviets 58 tanks and thousands of casualties, mostly due to inept tactics that saw armour advancing with no infantry support and rifle battalions charging en masse across open ground, straight into wire entanglements and the non-stop chatter of Finnish Maxim machine guns. As with Taipale, the Soviet efforts burned themselves out for no gain but with great loss, leaving the defenders bruised but elated. Less than six weeks later, however, it was clear to the Finns that another offensive was on the way, the Soviets making little attempt to hide the fact that once again the road to Viipuri would be the main objective of Timoshenko's revitalized Red Army.

MAP KEY

1 February: A series of attacks, started on 1 February, culminate in Army Commander (1st rank) Timoshenko's main offensive on 11 February, the 100th Rifle Division being tasked with taking Summa while the 123rd Rifle Division is to seize 'Millionaire' and 'Poppius' bunkers on the road to Lähde.

2 1100hrs, 11 February: The 245th Rifle Regiment and the 255th Rifle Regiment, supported by at least two companies of tanks (one of T-28s, the other T-26s), attack towards 'Poppius' and 'Millionaire'. The attack towards Lieutenant H.V. Hannus' position, unsupported by armour because of the swampy ground, is repulsed with heavy loss of life.

3 1200–1400hrs, 11 February: The 245th Rifle Regiment attacks 'Poppius' bunker, which falls at approximately 1300hrs. Lieutenant Malm's 5/IR 9 falls back. With his flank exposed and a tank attack brewing, Lieutenant Hannus' company also falls back.

4 1100–1600hrs, 11 February: The 255th Rifle Regiment attacks 'Millionaire' bunker but is repulsed with heavy losses.

5 11/12 February: Through a series of concerted attacks the 255th Rifle Regiment manages to surround the now unsupported 'Millionaire' bunker; engineers dynamite the bunker at 0500hrs on 12 February (the Finns say 13 February), killing most of the remaining defenders. Lieutenant M.G. Ericsson's 4/IR 9, too weak to retake the shattered position, retreats.

6 13 February: The 245th Rifle Regiment supported by the 90th and 112th Tank battalions advances on the support line at Lähde, breaking through. The breach is one of the factors that forces the Finns to abandon the Mannerheim Line.

Battlefield environment

The 'Viipuri Gateway', described by writer Robert Edwards as 'the only accessible route through the Isthmus to the vulnerable Finnish interior…centred on the little village of Summa' (Edwards 2006: 108) was studded with defensive bunkers supported by a network of trenches that were in turn screened with minefields, wire entanglements and local boulders pressed into use as anti-tank obstacles. The key bunkers for the whole Summa–Lähde sector were 'Millionaire' (so called because of its great cost) to the west and 'Poppius' (named for its first commander) to the east. Colonel Philip Alyabushev, commander of the 123rd Rifle Division, described 'Millionaire' bunker as the Soviets saw it: 'This was the strongest fortification. It had hill Yazyk

(Tongue) behind it. Here the bunker had a form of caponier with gunports, from which one could fire from one side towards Summajarvi lake [to the west], and from the other – approaches to Hill 65.5 [the 'Poppius' bunker's position to the east]. At the same place a good observation post with two steel armored cupolas and several soil and wood bunkers were located. All fortifications of the enemy were connected to each other. They could only be captured simultaneously, as one bunker would cover the approaches to the next one' (Alyabushev Memoir). Both bunkers could house around a platoon of men and each was armed with a pair of heavy machine guns, as well as a single anti-tank gun (most likely the 37mm Bofors).

A small group of Finnish soldiers examine the remains of a bunker (possibly the western casemate of 'Poppius') in the Summa–Lähde sector in the summer of 1941. Both bunkers were extensively damaged during the Winter War, and suffered further destruction in the years afterwards. The landscape around the bunkers was dotted with trench lines and wooden machine-gun bunkers, and was lightly forested, though most of the area's trees were little more than broken or stunted poles at the time of Timoshenko's 11 February attack as a result of the massive Soviet artillery bombardments. (SA-kuva)

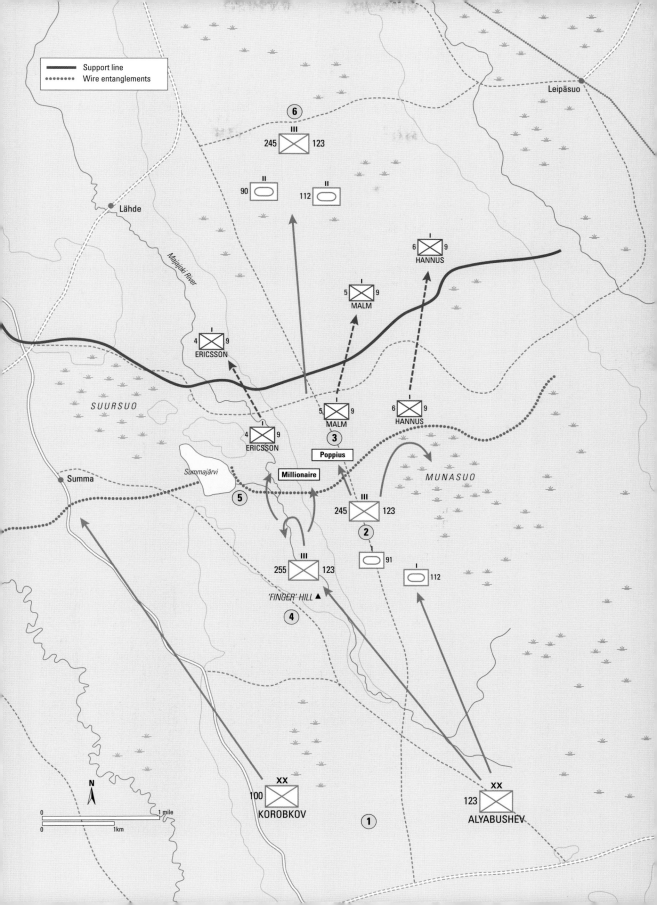

Support line
Wire entanglements

Leipäsuo

⑥

245 ⊠ 123

II
90 ▭

II
112 ▭

I
6 ⊠ 9
HANNUS

Lähde

Majajoki River

I
5 ⊠ 9
MALM

I
4 ⊠ 9
ERICSSON

SUURSUO

I
5 ⊠ 9
MALM

I
6 ⊠ 9
HANNUS

I
4 ⊠ 9
ERICSSON

Poppius

③

Summajärvi

MUNASUO

Summa

Millionaire

⑤

III
245 ⊠ 123

②

▭ 91

III
255 ⊠ 123

I
112 ▭

'FINGER' HILL ▲

④

N

0 _____ 1 mile
0 _____ 1km

XX
100 ⊠
KOROBKOV

①

XX
123 ⊠
ALYABUSHEV

INTO COMBAT

For the Finns in the Karelian Isthmus, January 1940 had been a trying time. The Soviets had kept up the pressure all along the line, with an unending succession of artillery bombardments, air attacks and infantry assaults wearing down the defending battalions, and depleting even further the Finnish artillery force's dwindling stock of shells. The insistency of such blows increased dramatically on 1 February as the first stage of Timoshenko's new offensive began. Artillery strikes grew in number and intensity, and major attacks were launched at various points all along the line in an attempt to disguise where the hammer-blow would eventually fall. The bunker system in the Viipuri Gateway was subject to increasingly effective fire, with the Soviets bringing up heavy guns which caused significant damage to 'Poppius' (Poppiuslinnake: 'Fort of Poppius') and 'Millionaire' (Miljoonalinnake: 'Millionaire fort'), the two most modern of the Finnish strongpoints, the defeat of which would be the key to any successful Soviet armoured thrust in the Summa area. The western casemate of 'Millionaire' had been wrecked on 28 January, and its central observation tower destroyed as well, a jury-rigged periscope taking its place.

Battalion-sized Soviet infantry assaults well supported by armour were common, with several of the Finns' smaller strongpoints and wooden bunkers either being destroyed or changing hands several times in the see-sawing battles that raged up and down the length of the line. Despite such pressure, some among the Finnish command seemed surprisingly sanguine about the nature of the Soviet incursions, perhaps in part because in the earlier phase of the war such assaults had always burned themselves out after the attacking divisions had ground themselves down to the bone against bunker walls. This time, however, was different. Soviet rifle battalions that had been decimated in an attack were rotated out of the line, their place taken by a fresh unit ready for the next assault, so the pressure against the line was not going to weaken. The Finns could not hope to do the same, their troops having to suffer weeks of intensive fighting without any significant rest or relief. Indeed on 11 February, the day Timoshenko's offensive started in earnest, that pressure would fast become unbearable.

Summa and Lähde were the responsibility of II Corps' 3rd Division, which had been on the line throughout the weeks of Soviet punishment. General Harald Öhquist, commander of II Corps, noted that 'the men of the Third Division are dead tired and absolutely must be relieved' (quoted in Trotter 2003: 218), but the only available unit – 5th Division – was the key reserve for the whole line, so the 3rd Division stayed where it was. Local relief would have to suffice, so the infantry battalion at the head of the line, I/IR 8, was pulled out the evening before the main Soviet attack, and replaced with II/IR 9 under the command of Major Arthur Lindman, which was almost as poorly off as the unit it was replacing. Though fresher than I/IR 8, it counted fewer than 400 men out of a peacetime complement of around 1,000; it had not operated on this part of the front before, and had very little experience of dealing with Soviet tank attacks. What was more, it was entirely Swedish-speaking; not a problem in the normal run of things (many Finns spoke the language), but at a time of intense stress it made the risks of miscommunication all the greater. The regiment's three rifle companies had to cover almost 2.5km

A Finnish 122mm H/09 or H/10 howitzer, packed for transport across the snow. The Finns had shortages of all types of artillery, but the relative paucity of heavy pieces was a constant problem. Thus it was a disaster when, on 13 February 1940, the Soviet 90th and 112th Tank battalions broke through the line at Lähde and quickly came upon the position of the Finnish 2nd Heavy Artillery Battalion, which was caught completely by surprise. The artillerymen ran for their lives, abandoning their 150mm H/14j howitzers, 11 of which were captured by the Soviets within minutes. Only one such gun, away from the front for repairs, avoided capture. The artillerymen mostly scattered, but 32 of them sought refuge in a bunker, refusing to surrender. The Soviets, in no mood for a drawn-out parley, set charges and destroyed the bunker, killing all the men within it. (SA-kuva)

of front; 5/IR 9 under Lieutenant Malm occupied the positions around 'Poppius' bunker covering the Lähde road, while 4/IR 9 under Lieutenant M.G. Ericsson was to the west occupying 'Millionaire' bunker and Lieutenant H.V. Hannus had 6/IR 9 positioned to the east behind the Munasuo swamp.

In the darkness opposite, the rifle regiments of the 123rd Rifle Division under the command of Colonel Philip Alyabushev spent the early-morning hours of Sunday 11 February in preparation. Alyabushev was fresh to the division but had made a strong impression; the staff officer Captain Nazarov noted how 'I have no idea if he had any sleep at all, but he was always at the front and bitched about even the smallest detail. He achieved extremely high levels of readiness in his troops' (quoted in Irincheev 2011: 125). Two of the division's rifle regiments, the 245th (under Sub-Colonel Rosly) and 255th, had been involved in the December attacks on Summa, and both had been bloodily rebuffed from the 'Millionaire' and 'Poppius' bunkers with great loss of life. Now they had been brought back up to strength and re-equipped with better, warmer clothes than those they had suffered in during December, some troops even being issued with winter camouflage. The 123rd Rifle Division had been chosen to lead the initial attack against the Finnish bunkers, and the officers and men had spent weeks practising dummy attacks against mocked-up fortifications in anticipation; morale was high, with an eager fighting spirit evident among the men. The 245th Rifle Regiment, including II/245 RR under Captain Soroka, was allotted two companies of tanks in support (one of T-28s from the 91st Tank Battalion under Lieutenant Kharaborkin, the other of T-26s from the 112th Tank Battalion); it was tasked with taking 'Poppius' bunker in the centre of the Finnish line, while its sister unit, the 255th Rifle Regiment, would simultaneously strike at 'Millionaire' bunker on the Soviet left flank. Both regiments were to have their battalions attack in echelon, allowing no breathing-space for the defenders.

Overall, 300,000 artillery shells would be fired on the Karelian front that day. Lieutenant Viktor M. Iskrov, a platoon leader with the 68th Independent Mortar

Battery that was equipped with the 120mm M1938 mortar, worked with elements of the 100th Rifle Division (who would be attacking Summa village to the west) and the 123rd Rifle Division in the run-up to the main offensive:

> I do not remember in which division we were – maybe in the 123rd? We were always transferred from one division to another … My direct commander was Moskalenko, and he would say: now you go to this division, get in touch with commander of this regiment … This is how I always worked at the front line with a company or with a battalion. I mention the battalion because sometimes there was very little left of the companies. There used to be losses when a Rifle Regiment would have eleven men left from the original number of 1800. (Iskrov Interview)

Lieutenant Iskrov recalled the initial bombardment, which began at 0840hrs and continued unabated until 1100hrs:

> On February 11, 1940, there was a very strong artillery fire, we hit them hard. There were pine trees on the Millionaire bunker, some forty years old. They were also all knocked down by our artillery. Our task was to open the Millionaire bunker from sand, stones and soil, knock down the trees and so on. Then the infantry moved forward. (Iskrov Interview)

The immensity of the attack shocked Major Lindman into insensibility, leaving his lieutenants to fend for themselves in the coming fight. The two Soviet rifle regiments streamed towards the bunkers, where both sites were quickly engaged in a ferocious fight. Private Rafael Forth of 4/IR 9 was among those defending 'Millionaire' bunker:

> The Russians did not shoot so much at the bunker itself, but assaulted to the right from the bunker at the so-called Finger Hill. The 4th Company tried to mop up the trenches with hand grenades and submachine-gun fire, but it was in vain. The Russians took a good hold on the hill and were coming closer and closer to the bunker through the trenches. Simultaneously with the Russian infantry approaching the right entrance, a Russian tank drove straight at the bunker, most likely with a plan to block the left entrance. Now it was time for the AT gun to act … the gun fired many shells that had tracers, but the tank was just coming closer and closer to us. It was only when the tank was 150–200 metres away that our AT gun managed to score a direct hit. The tank stalled and started burning. (Quoted in Irincheev 2011: 127–28)

Knocking out the tank did not slow the Soviet attack, as machine-gun fire saturated the bunker and the men of the 255th Rifle Regiment worked their way through the trench line to the top of the bunker itself, where it took a shower of hand grenades followed by submachine-gun fire to clear them off again, forcing them back into the trenches.

On the eastern flank behind the Munasuo swamp, Lieutenant Hannus and 6/IR 9 sat in relative safety; the swamp denied the Soviet armour a chance to get near them, leaving the job to the infantry alone. Wave after wave of them came on, each to be cut down in their turn by machine-gun fire from Hannus' men, leading the Soviets to nickname the whole area as 'the valley of

Red Army pioneers at work. Such units found themselves in high demand as death and injury resulting from exploding booby traps provided an unwelcome surprise for the Soviets from the very first days of the campaign. Dmitrii Krutskikh well remembers the problems they caused: 'We didn't know Finnish landmines – we would stumble upon one of them and study it, until somebody gets blown to pieces. Sometimes we were just lucky. The Finns used English-made anti-personnel mines, the ones they later started making themselves. Besides, they also put artillery projectiles right into field obstacles. Fields in front of wire obstacles were also densely mined, they put mines right into snow, set up booby-traps. The mining density was very high. Doors in villages were also booby-trapped. At first, our scouts were getting blown up. But, come January, we began fighting differently … We also acquired some kind of sense for these mines. When you look at the snow at first, you see only an even surface, but after a while you discern little bumps. You look in your binoculars, then send in the scouts – indeed, landmines are there' (Krutskikh Interview). (Photo by ullstein bild/ullstein bild via Getty Images)

death'. Unsupported attacks would not by themselves be able to dislodge 6/IR 9, but the attack of the 245th Rifle Regiment at the centre of the line was about to change the picture for all concerned.

At 'Poppius' bunker, Lieutenant Malm's men had started the fight well. Accurate fire cut down the first wave of Soviet troops, but Soroka's II/245 RR immediately took up the fight, advancing with tank support. Four of the tanks were knocked out on the approach, but there were simply too many of them for the Finns to stop:

> This was not a new tactic; when it had been tried before, the bunker's garrison had called for fire from the Bofors guns or had sneaked out the rear entrance and plastered the vehicles with [Molotov] cocktails and grenade bundles. It was not possible to do that now. The Russians had improved their tank–infantry tactics to the point where each vehicle was adequately covered by men with automatic weapons, and every single gun in the Lähde sector was out of action, not from direct hits but from concussion. (Trotter 2003: 228)

The inability to fend off the Soviet tanks was proving to be a serious problem as dozens of them were firing on 'Poppius' bunker unopposed, while others were manoeuvring right up to the bunker's embrasures, blocking the defenders' fields of fire. With the Finns forced outside to fight in the open, a desperate melee began, with the defenders using hand grenades and all the small arms at their disposal to keep the attackers at bay. At least one Soviet company was practically wiped out in the assault, and hundreds more were killed and wounded within 100m of the bunker, but the weight of numbers coupled with their armoured support overwhelmed the position; at 1328hrs the Red Banner was raised over the ruins. Lieutenant Malm and his shattered company fought on for another hour until both he and his remaining men, unable to retake the position they had lost, withdrew to the support line. Of the 100 men of 5/IR 9 who had moved into the position the previous day, a mere 16 were left.

The collapse of the centre of the line was a critical moment for the whole Soviet advance. The Red Banner was flying above the wrecked 'Poppius'

A patrol of Finns due to set out near the end of the war. The soldier in the centre carries a 7.62mm Lahti-Saloranta M/26, one of the standard Finnish LMGs of the war; the man to his left carries a 7.62mm AVS-36 rifle (identifiable by the large muzzle brake used to reduce recoil), while the man on the right carries a 7.62mm SVT-38 rifle, both captured from the Soviets. Neither rifle worked particularly well, especially not when subjected to the rigours of front-line use. The AVS-36 was overly complex, making maintenance difficult, while the SVT-38 had a host of shortcomings, not the least of which was the fact that it was poorly made. Both weapons were used in the early days of the Great Patriotic War, but by that stage they had been superseded by the 7.62mm SVT-40. (SA-kuva)

bunker, surrounded by jubilant riflemen; and the tanks, now freed from supporting them, began to move down the Lähde road with the apparent aim of enveloping the right flank of Hannus' position behind the swamp, forcing him to pull his company back to the support line and out of immediate danger. With the centre and left flanks of the Finnish line crumbling, only Ericsson's position in and around 'Millionaire' bunker remained. Junior Lieutenant Lekanov had been put in charge of one of the 255th Rifle Regiment's assault parties. Held in reserve, he waited and watched as two of his comrades took their own assault troops towards 'Millionaire', only to see them caught in defensive obstacles and pinned down by heavy fire. Called into action, he began his advance:

> We walked out of the forest towards the hill and were immediately hit by mortar fire. We crawled towards the trenches with heavy boxes of explosives. I ordered my soldiers to take off their white overalls, as they only made it easier to spot us against the black background of soil ploughed by artillery fire … The White Finns locked themselves in their underground fortress. We crawled on the roof of the bunker with the boxes of explosives. (Quoted in Irincheev 2011: 131)

The Soviet assault party realized that they did not have enough explosives with them to reduce the fortress, but there was enough to blow up one of the

A Finn examines a Red Army bunker in Kuhmo on 14 March 1940, a day after the war's end. He is immediately identifiable as a Finn by the *puukko* knife attached to his belt. Such knives were ubiquitous, but they were not issued by the Finnish Army – each man was responsible for supplying his own. As such they came in a bewildering variety of sizes and finishes, though they all shared common characteristics such as a fixed single-edged blade, no guard, and handles and sheaths often worked into elaborate designs. As general-purpose tools of woodsmen, *puukko* knives were not designed for combat, though they were certainly used in that way; there is no clear sense of how common such usage was, nor how effective they proved to be, but anecdotally at least the Soviets feared them, perhaps for the silent death they symbolized as much as anything else. (SA-kuva)

entrances to the bunker, helping to trap the defenders inside and allowing Red Army riflemen to flood around all sides of the position, surrounding it entirely. By this time there were only eight Finns left inside, under the command of Lieutenant Skade. There is some confusion in the sources as to the exact sequence of events that followed, including the eventual destruction of 'Millionaire', with the Soviets stating that they destroyed it on the morning of 12 February, while the Finns claim it was the morning of the following day. Whichever version is true, a relief party from Infantry Regiment 8 was sent to try to free the men trapped inside, but the weight of fire laid down by the Soviets was too great.

A group of three men managed to slip out and make it back to Finnish lines, but Private Forth, who left in the company of a pair of runners who had told everyone to evacuate, was caught by the Soviets. He was shocked at the sight that greeted him as he was taken back towards the Soviet lines: thousands

Firefight at 'Millionaire' Bunker

Finnish view: A small party of Finns from 4/IR 9, some from the bunker and others from the defensive trenches, advance onto the eastern casemate of 'Millionaire' to stop the Soviets from gaining control of both the east and west entrances. The Finns, mostly armed with SMGs and supported by a 7.62mm Lahti-Saloranta M/26 LMG, are laying down heavy fire that sees Soviet soldiers falling left and right. Colonel Philip Alyabushev, commander of the 123rd Rifle Division, noted how earlier attacks launched by the division against this section of the Summa–Lähde line in December 1939 were 'carried out ... without proper preparation. Why do I say without proper preparation? Lack of preparation was expressed in lack of cooperation between the different combat arms, each combat arm acted independently, and as [a] result we had very high casualties of armor, while the fortified area was not broken through' (Alyabushev Memoir). Such coordination was not lacking this time, with ferocious artillery support together with concerted attacks by tanks that were usually carried out in concert with infantry; but despite relatively quick – if costly – success at 'Poppius' bunker to the east, 'Millionaire' bunker would prove to be a tougher nut to crack.

Soviet view: The men of the 255th Rifle Regiment, after working their way up 'Finger' Hill, have made it to the top of 'Millionaire's' western embrasure and are charging towards the eastern casemate in the open. They are being cut down by fire from SMGs and an LMG. A 7.62mm DP-28 LMG crew work feverishly to get their jammed gun working again. A team of assault engineers work to block the entrances of the western casemate. Private Rafael Forth of 4/IR 9 remembered how 'The Russians advanced through the trenches from the Finger to the right entrance [the western casemate]. They climbed the roof of the bunker from there and took defensive positions ... Ericsson gave an order to storm the roof of the bunker from the left [eastern] entrance ... I was unscrewing the lids on the stick grenades and passing them on to Gunnar. He threw them on as fast as he could, so that the grenades exploded on the roof. After we threw all the stick grenades on the roof, the guys from the 4th Company stormed the roof. They "wiped the roof clean" with submachine-guns and light MGs' (quoted in Irincheev 2011: 128–29).

of soldiers and masses of armour that left him thinking it would only be a matter of time before such men were parading through Helsinki. Lieutenant Skade and the three remaining men still in the bunker made an attempt to break out but quickly ran into a group of Soviet soldiers, forcing them to retreat back into 'Millionaire' and block the doors. Calls for them to surrender were followed by showers of Soviet hand grenades through the gun ports, but the trapped Finns refused to buckle.

Junior Lieutenant Lekanov, whose assault party had played such an important role in breaking into the bunker, was now tasked with its destruction:

> we took the boxes with explosives from the trenches and laid them on top of the left [western] casemate. A huge pile of boxes with explosives grew on top of the bunker. The infantry withdrew to the trenches. Fuses were lit at my command. A tremendous explosion. A huge flame shot into the sky. We were all covered up with soil. Ears were ringing for a long time, our heads were spinning. We walked to the site of the explosion … there was a crater up to 10 metres in diameter. The iron reinforcement vanished into dust. Everything was blackened 50 metres from the explosion site. The huge bunker, along with its garrison, ceased to exist. This was at 0500 hours, 12 February 1940. (Quoted in Irincheev 2011: 132)

Astonishingly enough one of the Finns inside 'Millionaire', Gunnar Storm, survived the colossal detonation, and, though severely wounded, managed to crawl out of the ruins and into captivity. Lieutenant Iskrov observed the horrible scene that was left after the fighting:

> I had not personally seen the previous infantry assaults on that bunker. But there were a lot of dead bodies around it, including burnt-down corpses – apparently, they were burnt with a flame thrower. There were also detached parts of bodies, like legs and hands lying around. I should tell you straight that there were a lot of dead bodies. All the area of Summa–Hottinen was destroyed and smashed by artillery. There were only stumps left from the forest. Artillery was firing very well, they did not think about saving ammo. (Iskrov Interview)

The entire area had been blasted by shellfire, with the ground churned up for kilometre after kilometre, trees reduced to nothing more than stumps across the entire battlefield. Lieutenant Ericsson and his remaining men held their final positions for the rest of the morning, but by 1200hrs they too had pulled back to the support line. The Finnish companies had lost half their strength in the fight for the bunkers, while the Soviets certainly numbered their casualties in the thousands.

With 'Millionaire' and 'Poppius' lost, the road to the Finnish hinterland was open. There were no more anti-tank guns in the sector, nothing with which to mount an effective defence against a concerted Soviet armoured attack, especially not one where the closeness of supporting infantry denied the Finnish tank hunters a chance to get near enough to inflict any damage. Communications had been severely impeded by the artillery barrage which cut telephone wires and destroyed the phone junction at Lähde. Major Lindman, the most senior officer on that part of the line, had been broken by the initial

Finnish officers inspect one of the ruined bunkers in the Summa–Lähde sector in 1941. Life in the bunkers, even the ones designed to house their defenders in relative comfort, was unpleasant, and could be terrifying during combat. One veteran recalled: 'Black concrete bunkers stood in sparse forests without any communication cables or trenches. They were an intolerable place to be in combat, one had to always be ready to bail out immediately. Despite their high cost, they were hopeless rat holes and I am wondering why the enemy did not fry them all. If these bunkers were equipped with anti-tank weapons, one could defend oneself against tanks. In reality, all we could do was sit inside the bunker and wait for a tank to drive up and do what he pleased' (quoted in Nenye, Munter & Wirtanen 2015: 84). (SA-kuva)

barrage and was of no use in communicating with his subordinates or higher command. The general confusion caused by the scale and intensity of the fight would have strained an effective and well-maintained network, so it was no surprise that vital information about the developing Soviet breakthrough was not getting back to the Finnish command in an accurate or timely manner. As a result the 5th Division – the only force in the area capable of plugging the terrible hole that been opened up in the Mannerheim Line – was slow off the mark, giving the Soviets time to consolidate their gains and dig in.

The Soviet divisions could have pushed on, but practicalities were beginning to get in the way. The losses incurred during the breakthrough had been severe, and fresh units would be needed to exploit the gap in the Finnish line, but such forces were not yet properly organized. The rest of the Karelian Isthmus had taken a similarly ferocious beating from the Red Army, but it was only at Summa and Lähde that breakthroughs of any significance were achieved. Nevertheless, the bringing to bear of massive Soviet military power on thinning and worn-down Finnish forces was the pattern of things to come. A Finnish counter-attack against the Lähde salient was launched on 12 February, with a more concerted effort by four infantry battalions set in motion on 13 February; but despite making some headway the response was too late, and the forces making it were too weak, especially in the face of repeated interdiction by the thunderously powerful Soviet artillery. The Finnish historian Wolf H. Halsti was a member of the 5th Division and an eyewitness to the failed counter-attack: 'The tactical situation is and of itself *not* hopeless! Only the means to deal with it are lacking! If only we had some heavy weapons!' (quoted in Trotter 2003: 230).

Analysis

The purges inflicted on the Red Army had a shattering impact on combat effectiveness. The publicist Ernst Henri, in a letter to Soviet writer Ilya Ehrenburg, put the cost succinctly: 'No defeat has ever led to such monstrous losses in command personnel. Only the complete surrender of a nation after a lost war could have such a rout as a consequence' (quoted in Glantz 1998: 32). The damage to the officer corps and the impact that had on training and doctrine meant that the Red Army of 1939 was a mechanized army that did not have the skill or experience to fight a mechanized war. That such an army was tasked with invading a country which in almost every respect offered a disastrously poor environment for vehicles of any kind, wheeled or tracked, did not help. Logistics were a major problem, with the supply lines from Leningrad suffering less from the absolute distance that had to be travelled than from the poor condition of the lands through which they stretched. Such problems were compounded by corruption, lazy planning, incompetence and a lack of forethought, Langdon-Davies observing of the Soviets that 'They did not bring with them the things they ought to have brought, and they brought with them the things they ought to have left behind' (Langdon-Davies 1941: 11). The Finns, fighting on their own ground using their preferred tactics against a long-expected foe, were as well prepared for the war as they could reasonably hope to be.

Overall, despite the apparent strength of the Soviet assault on the Karelian Isthmus, the Soviet forces were too weak to guarantee a breakthrough, or successfully exploit one if it came. Their initial line was six divisions strong, the same as that of the defending Finns, and their major advantage – overwhelming numbers of tanks and artillery – was hamstrung by local conditions, dismal logistics and hopelessly poor tactical performance. A disorderly lack of cohesion between the different arms of service seemed to be the norm as opposed to the exception. Marshal Mannerheim's observation that the Red Army was like a 'badly conducted orchestra in which instruments

A soldier from a Finnish ski patrol in Märkäjärvi, 14 February 1940, carrying a 7.65mm Bergmann M/20 SMG slung around his neck. The Finns' use of SMGs such as the Bergmann and especially the 9mm Suomi KP/31 SMG became one of the lessons of the Winter War. Though they were never available in the numbers required, they proved to be very effective in the hands of the men who were trained to use them, particularly in the hit-and-run tactics employed against Soviet columns and encircled positions. Soviet Lieutenant Dmitrii Krutskikh noted how he and his men were forbidden from using them – or any other – captured equipment: 'We got hold of a Suomi when we took Khiliki … But we had a very strict order – not to take anything off the dead. Everything had to be turned in! However, when we took defense, then we used them. I fired a Suomi myself. It's a good gun but very heavy. It hangs on your neck like a log. Anyway, the submachine gun's strength is in its impact on the enemy's morale' (Krutskikh Interview). (SA-kuva)

were played out of time' (quoted in Bozek 1993: 27) sums up such Soviet failings rather succinctly.

The attacks on Taipale were costly, and though the initial river crossings allowed a foothold on the northern bank, it was in an area that the Finns had already decided was indefensible, and over which they had spent much time plotting artillery strikes and laying out interweaving fields of machine-gun fire. The numerical advantage in infantry enjoyed by the Red Army was significant, but not enough on its own to force the issue. A more effective use of artillery to suppress the Finnish line, and in particular better coordination between tanks and infantry, may well have engendered much better results. Attacks, often planned rapidly and without much depth of thought, were carried out at great cost in men and *matériel*, and were blunted by conventional defensive tactics. The local conditions and terrain seemed to play little part in the thinking of senior Red Army commanders, and their forces suffered accordingly.

It can be argued that the attacks in northern Finland were unnecessary. Any success enjoyed by the 9th or 14th armies would be largely pointless if the southern thrust to Viipuri failed. Difficult to supply and of limited strategic value, the Soviet divisions (particularly the mechanized ones) bogged down in the wintry horror of Finnish forests would probably have been of much more use in the Karelian Isthmus. Nevertheless, the attempt to cut Finland in two might have borne some strategic fruit, but after the first fortnight's fighting any such outcome looked increasingly fanciful. That the general thrust of the Soviet attack remained unchanged even as minor reverses started to become major disasters, exposed a lack of imagination among the divisional, corps and army commanders that would have appalling consequences.

Questioned about the failure of the 44th Rifle Division, Captain Pastukhov, commander of II/146 RR – one of the few battalions to make it back to Soviet lines as a functioning unit – stated that 'the main reason for our defeat was that the regiment was split in battalions and battalions were split in companies, which fought independently' (quoted in Irincheev 2011: 117). In hindsight the Soviet tactic of spreading the divisional forces thinly to be able to dig in along the length of the road seems tailor-made to invite exactly the sort of tactics the Finns most wanted to use, namely cutting the line at numerous points along its length and strangling the resulting pockets, one after the other. The Raate Road offered the Finnish fighter almost everything he could hope for – a perfect environment for his preferred tactics, with the time to put them to work against an enemy that could only react, it seemed, never initiate.

The motorized nature of the 44th Rifle Division was an obvious problem in an environment where there was only one poor main road with no possibility of employing lateral columns or even an effective reconnaissance screen. It was clearly the wrong tool for the job, and the blame for that must lie with the men who planned the Soviet attack in such an arrogant and slapdash manner. These problems were exacerbated by the division's inability to adapt itself in any way to local conditions, more or less allowing its elements to be pulled taut along a thin road in hostile territory, at the mercy of the elements, and the Finns who knew how to exploit them. Vinogradov's apparent paralysis in the face of even minor setbacks or enemy action surrendered all initiative to the Finns, who made much of such a valuable gift. Brave and tenacious though many of the Soviet riflemen proved to be, their broken-backed command doomed the majority of their efforts. The success of the Finns, remarkable though it was, owed a great deal to the failings of their enemy.

At the Viipuri Gateway the Red Army seemed, in some respects at least, to have come a long way in a short time when Timoshenko launched his attack in the Karelian Isthmus on 1 February 1940. Coordination between tanks and infantry was better, with examples of riflemen offering close support and in some cases riding into battle on the tanks themselves, making the job of the Finnish tank-hunting units much harder. The use of artillery was much more effective, and not simply as a result of having more guns with which to work; barrages were concentrated more effectively, specific sections of the Finnish line (including bunkers, wire entanglements and timber strongpoints) were targeted and effectively wrecked before the main attacks went in, and there was much better communication with units calling for fire support. The sheer weight of the new assault helped to mitigate tactical failings and operational blunders, though still at a horribly high cost in men and *matériel*, but it was a cost that Timoshenko, a man not burdened by undue concern for the lives of his soldiers, was happy to pay. The riflemen, the backbone of the Red Army, fought on, and fought well. Reese observed that, despite the terrible setbacks,

A selection of rather phlegmatic Soviet prisoners, taken in Parikkala early in the war. Despite the fact that the Soviet Union committed over 900,000 men to the war, only 5,486 surrendered to the Finns, a surprisingly small number considering the scale of some the Red Army's defeats and the brutal conditions that its soldiers had to endure. Nevertheless the prospects for such men would prove to be exceedingly grim, for they fought for a system that punished any failure, real or perceived, with vindictive fervour. Reese notes that 'Of the over 5,000 Red Army men captured by the Finns who were repatriated in 1940, 350 were summarily executed and 4,354 were sentenced to hard labor in the camps for terms of five to eight years' (Reese 2008: 833). Though the war barely lasted three months, the relative toll it had taken was severe; the butcher's bill was steep for both sides, but especially so for the Soviets. According to Reese, 'the Red Army is estimated to have lost 131,476 dead and missing, 264,908 wounded and injured, 132,213 frostbitten, and 5,486 captured (534,083 total) out of over 900,000 men involved in the war (just under 60 percent casualties). The Finns lost around 22,430 killed and missing, 43,357 wounded, and 847 soldiers captured by the Soviets. A further 1,029 Finnish civilians were killed' (Reese 2008: 830). (SA-kuva)

> the army overall as an institution, the forces in the theater of operations, and most if not a majority of individual soldiers never lost the desire to overcome the foe; unit cohesion, although seriously challenged, remained for the most part intact, while morale waned and wavered but never collapsed; the soldiers' investment (interest) in the success of the mission never failed; and discipline, if sometimes tenuous, did not give way. (Reese 2008: 826)

For the Finns there was a perhaps understandable complacency in the face of the Soviet attacks during 1–10 February 1940, as they assumed that the game had not changed all that much from December 1939. The vigour and consistency of Soviet attacks along the whole line for ten days straight – twice the length of the previous year's battles at Summa and Kelja – as well as the barely concealed nature of their troop and artillery build-up were clear indications that something different was on the way. That said, even if they were waiting for the Soviets on tenterhooks it is difficult to see what significant step the Finns could have taken to thwart an attack that was so massive and unforgiving: with their ranks depleted and worn out by weeks of incessant fighting they did not have the men, the anti-tank guns, the artillery pieces or the ammunition to stem the Soviet tide. The disparity between the two forces was simply too great.

Aftermath

The Finns had lost the war but won a reputation. Their stubborn independence (and the international renown such pluck engendered) probably went a long way to persuading Stalin that complete occupation of all Finland – his likely initial desire – would cast him in a rather villainous light on the world stage; not so much liberator as grasping bully. It is probable that, had Finland acquiesced to Stalin's initial demands, he would have attempted to take the rest of the country the following year, in the same manner as he did with the helpless Baltic States. Finland's loss secured her independence but not her security, so it was to some degree understandable that she would throw in her lot with Germany when the chance came to retake lost lands and push back the Soviet shadow under which the country had laboured for more than two decades.

The frankly catastrophic failures of the Red Army in the Winter War had severe consequences, both internally and abroad. The embarrassments of the campaign prompted a more serious attempt at military reform, but in a regime in which bad news could be ignored and those deemed to have fallen short made ready scapegoats, such reforms were both slow and haphazard. There was a general assumption within the higher echelons of the Soviet command that sooner or later there would be war with Germany, but they considered any action before 1942 quite unlikely. As the Red Army reforms were due to be completed in 1942, one wonders if the Soviets were relying on the idea that the Germans would not have the bad manners to start a war until the Soviet Union was ready to fight it.

Just as significantly, the Red Army's dismal showing offered much encouragement to Hitler and the Japanese in their designs on the Soviet Union; starved through most of the 1930s of any real sense of just how such a vast military machine might work in practice, the Soviets' broken leadership, inadequate levels of equipment and generally poor troop performance came as a welcome shock. 'Their consequent conclusion that

Stalin had fatally weakened his defensive forces persuaded them to take chances that a strong and experienced Soviet officer corps might have discouraged' (Habeck 2002: 95). They tended to overlook the fact that the Red Army had only committed a moderate portion of its still-growing strength to the Finnish campaign, and that the horrendous casualties suffered – which would have been a national catastrophe for any Western army – were absorbed without any significant effort.

Lastly, they overlooked the fact that, initial disasters aside, the Red Army won the war. Marshal Mannerheim, in conversation with Erfurth later in World War II, observed that 'In the Winter War of 1939–40 the poor showing of the Russians was not camouflage; it was the true picture' (Erfurth 1951: 20). But it was not the whole picture. Reese notes that 'by all objective indices of its preparedness in the months leading up to the war and during the first six weeks of fighting, [the Red Army] might have been expected to collapse against a competent foe that could thwart its advance, defeat its attacks, and inflict the number of casualties the Finns did. Yet it did not collapse' (Reese 2011: 29). Reese's argument – that the Red Army remained a force to be reckoned with because it never lost the will to win, unit cohesion remained mostly intact, morale did not collapse, the investment of the ordinary Red Army man in victory did not fail, and discipline did not give way – is well reasoned and compelling (Reese 2011: 28–29). For all its failings, catastrophes and embarrassments, the Red Army wanted victory and had the brute strength to achieve it.

UNIT ORGANIZATIONS

Finnish

By the war's close, Finland had fielded ten infantry divisions of various shapes and sizes in three corps, as well as numbers of smaller forces and independent units. The standard composition of such a division was not notably different from that fielded by other countries at this time. At full strength it would be made up of 14,200 men, consisting of a headquarters element, three infantry regiments, an artillery regiment of three battalions (each battalion having one four-gun battery of 122mm howitzers and two four-gun batteries of 76mm field guns), a light detachment (consisting of a mix of two Jäger, cavalry or bicycle companies and a machine-gun platoon), two engineer companies, two signal companies, and a detached anti-tank-gun company (though most divisions did not have one of the latter before February 1940).

An infantry regiment (2,954 men at full strength) consisted of a headquarters section (12 men), three infantry battalions (845 men) and a mortar company (83 men and four 81mm or 82mm mortars). Each infantry battalion consisted of an HQ section (six men), a Jäger platoon, three rifle companies (191 men each) and a machine-gun company (154 men and 12 HMGs). Rifle companies had a headquarters element (15 men) and four rifle platoons of 38 men each (HQ of four men, two ten-man rifle squads each with one SMG-armed soldier, and two seven-man LMG squads) and a supply platoon (24 men).

A Jäger battalion had a battalion HQ, three Jäger companies, a machine-gun company and a gun company (made up of an anti-tank-gun platoon with two 37 PstK/36s, an infantry-gun platoon with two 37 K/15 Rosenberg infantry guns, and a mortar platoon with two 81mm or 82mm mortars). A Jäger company was made up of a headquarters group and three 38-man platoons that followed the same pattern as those of regular infantry. Sissi battalions – light guerrilla troops that specialized in fighting in the rough snowy terrain of central and northern Finland – had three companies, each with three rifle platoons (three ten-man rifle squads each with one SMG-armed soldier, and an *ahkio* team per platoon), an LMG platoon (two or four LMGs) and a signals platoon.

Soviet

The Soviet rifle division, usually organized into rifle corps of two or more divisions, fielded 18,881 men when at full strength, but most seemed to be closer to 14,000–15,000 in practice. The official structure in September 1939 was as follows: divisional headquarters (187 men), a signals battalion (312 men), a reconnaissance battalion (328 men), three infantry regiments (4,035 men each), one light-artillery regiment (1,898 men in three gun battalions: one of 12 76mm field guns and two of 12 122mm howitzers), one medium artillery regiment (1,303 men in two battalions: one of 12 122mm howitzers and one of 12 152mm howitzers), an anti-aircraft battalion (352 men and 12 anti-aircraft guns), an anti-tank battalion (282 men and 18 45mm anti-tank guns), a pioneer battalion (600 men) and various support and administrative units. Some divisions also retained an integral tank battalion (two companies of T-26 tanks, one of T-37 tanks).

A rifle regiment (4,035 men) had a headquarters section (67 men), two scout platoons (103 men each), a signal company (104 men), three rifle battalions (992 men each), an anti-tank battery (66 men and six 45mm anti-tank guns), an infantry-gun battery (159 men and six 76mm infantry guns), a mortar battery (41 men and four 120mm mortars), an anti-aircraft company (52 men with three quad-Maxims and six HMGs) and a pioneer and chemical platoon (85 men between them). A rifle battalion (992 men) was made up of a headquarters element (four men), a signal platoon (44 men), a scout platoon (62 men), three rifle companies (234 men each), a machine-gun company (94 men and 12 MMGs), a mortar platoon (18 men and four 82mm mortars), an anti-tank-gun platoon (18 men and two 45mm anti-tank guns), a pioneer squad (seven men) and the battalion train (43 men). Each rifle company (234 men) had a headquarters element (13 men), three rifle platoons (62 men each, made up of a command element of two men plus four 15-man rifle squads), a light-mortar section (11 men and three 50mm mortars) and a machine-gun platoon (22 men with two MMGs and two anti-tank rifles).

BIBLIOGRAPHY

44th Rifle Division War Diary. Excerpt from 20 December 1939 to 10 January 1940. http://web.archive.org/web/20110722065921/http://www.mannerheim-line.com/44th.htm (accessed 19 April 2016).

Ahlbäck, Anders (2014). *Manhood and the Making of the Military. Conscription, Military Service & Masculinity in Finland, 1917–39*. Farnham: Ashgate (ePUB e-book).

Alyabushev, Philip (no date). Memoir. http://web.archive.org/web/20080704172557/http://www.mannerheim-line.com/summa/assaultsj5.htm (accessed 19 April 2016).

Bozek, Gregory J. (1993). *The Soviet–Finnish War, 1939–1940. Getting the Doctrine Right*. Fort Leavenworth, KS: School of Advanced Military Studies. Available online at: http://cgsc.contentdm.oclc.org/cdm/singleitem/collection/p4013coll3/id/1417/rec/1 (accessed 6 June 2015).

Bull, Stephen (2013). *World War II Winter and Mountain Warfare Tactics*. Elite 193. Oxford: Osprey Publishing.

Chew, Allen F. (1980). 'Beating the Russians in Snow. The Finns and the Russians, 1940', in *Military Review*, June 1980: 38–47. http://cgsc.contentdm.oclc.org/cdm/singleitem/collection/p124201coll1/id/349/rec/1 (accessed 6 June 2015).

Chew, Allen F. (1981). *Fighting the Russians in Winter. Three Case Studies*. Leavenworth Papers No. 5. Fort Leavenworth, KS: Combat Studies Institute. http://cgsc.contentdm.oclc.org/cdm/singleitem/collection/p16040coll3/id/13/rec/1 (accessed 6 June 2015).

Chew, Allen F. (2007). *The White Death*. KiwE Publishing Ltd. Originally published in 1971 by Michigan State University Press.

Dunn, Walter S. (2009). *Hitler's Nemesis: The Red Army, 1930–45*. Mechanicsburg, PA: Stackpole Books.

Edwards, Robert (2006). *White Death: Russia's War on Finland 1939–40*. London: Weidenfeld & Nicolson.

Engle, Eloise & Paananen, Lauri (1992). *The Winter War: The Soviet Attack on Finland 1939–1940*. Mechanicsburg, PA: Stackpole Books.

Erfurth Waldemar (1951). *Warfare in the Far North*. Department of the Army Pamphlet No. 20-292. http://cgsc.contentdm.oclc.org/cdm/singleitem/collection/p4013coll9/id/368/rec/1 (retrieved 6 June 2015).

Fedyunin Memoir. http://militera.lib.ru/memo/russian/suomi/1_05.html (retrieved 1 April 2016).

Glantz, David M. (1998). *Stumbling Colossus: The Red Army on the Eve of World War*. Lawrence, KS: University Press of Kansas.

Habeck, Mary R. (2002). 'Dress Rehearsals, 1937–1941', in Robin Higham & Frederick Kagan, eds, *The Military History of the Soviet Union*. New York, NY: Palgrave: 93–107.

Irincheev, Bair & Delf, Brian (2013). *The Mannerheim Line 1920–39: Finnish Fortifications of the Winter War*. Fortress 88. Oxford: Osprey Publishing.

Irincheev, Bair (2011). *War of the White Death: Finland Against the Soviet Union 1939–40*. Barnsley: Pen & Sword Military.

Iskrov, Viktor M., Interview. http://web.archive.org/web/20090913003645/http://www.mannerheim-line.com/veterans/iskrove.htm (accessed 19 April 2016).

Jowett, Phillip S. (2006). *Finland at War 1939–45*. Elite 141. Oxford: Osprey Publishing.

Kagan, Frederick W. (2002). 'The Rise and Fall of Soviet Operational Art, 1917–1941', in Robin Higham & Frederick Kagan, eds, *The Military History of the Soviet Union*., New York, NY: Palgrave: 79–92.

Krutskikh, Dmitrii, Interview. http://iremember.ru/en/memoirs/infantrymen/dmitrii-krutskikh/ (accessed 19 April 2016).

Langdon-Davies, John (1941). *Invasion in the Snow: A Study of Mechanized War*. Boston, MA: Houghton Mifflin Co.

Merridale, Catherine (2005). *Ivan's War: The Red Army at War 1939–45*. London: Faber & Faber.

Nenye, Vesa, Munter, Peter & Wirtanen, Toni (2015). *Finland at War: The Winter War 1939–40*. Oxford: Osprey Publishing.

PU-36 (1986). *Provisional Field Regulations of the Red Army (JPRS-UMA-86-031)*. Springfield, VA: National Technical Information Service. handle.dtic.mil/100.2/ADA361873 (accessed 9 January 2016).

Reese, Roger R. (1996). *Stalin's Reluctant Soldiers: A Social History of the Red Army, 1925–1941*. Lawrence, KS: University Press of Kansas.

Reese, Roger R. (2008). 'Lessons of the Winter War: A Study in the Military Effectiveness of the Red Army, 1939–1940', in *The Journal of Military History*, Vol. 72, No. 3, July 2008, 825–52.

Reese, Roger R. (2011). *Why Stalin's Soldiers Fought: The Red Army's Military Effectiveness in World War II*. Lawrence, KS: University Press of Kansas.

Reese, Roger R. (2014). 'Stalin Attacks the Red Army', in *Military History Quarterly*, Autumn 2014, Vol. 27 No..1: 38–45.

Shilin, Aleksey: memoir. http://iremember.ru/memoirs/tankisti/shilin-aleksey-andreevich/ (accessed 19 April 2016).

Trotter, William R. (2003). *The Winter War: The Russo-Finnish War of 1939–40*. London: Aurum Press. New York, NY: Algonquin Books. Originally published 1991 in the USA under the title *A Frozen Hell: The Russo-Finish Winter War of 1939–40*.

Van Dyke, Carl (1997). *The Soviet Invasion of Finland, 1939–40*. Cass Series on Soviet Military Experience. London, Frank Cass.

Vehviläinen, Olli, trans. Gerard McAlester (2002). *Finland in the Second World War. Between Germany & Russia*. Basingstoke: Palgrave Macmillan.

Internet sources

Finnish Wartime Photograph Archive (http://sa-kuva.fi)

I Remember (http://www.iremember.ru)

Jaeger Platoon by Vihavainen, Jarkko: (http://www.jaegerplatoon.net)

Mannerheim-line, by Irincheev, Bair: (http://web.archive.org/web/20120205055855/http://www.mannerheim-line.com)

Militera (http://militera.lib.ru)

Mosin-Nagant by Snodgrass, Brent & Thomas, Vic: (http://www.mosinnagant.net/finland/default.asp)

RKKA (http://rkka.ru)

Winter War by Korhonen, Sami: (http://www.winterwar.com)

INDEX

References to illustrations are shown in **bold**. References to plates are shown in bold with caption pages in brackets, e.g. **38–39**, (40).